Bankers'
Lending Techniques

Bankers'
Lending Techniques

C N Rouse FCIB

The Chartered
Institute
of Bankers

First Published 1989

BANKERS BOOKS LIMITED
c/o The Chartered Institute of Bankers
10 Lombard Street
London EC3V 9AS

Chartered Institute of Bankers (CIB) Publications are published by Bankers Books Ltd under an exclusive licence and royalty agreement. Bankers Books Ltd is a company owned by the The Chartered Institute of Bankers.

ISBN 0 85297 228 8

 British Library Cataloguing in Publication Data

Rouse, C N
Bankers' Lending Techniques.
1. Great Britain. Lending by banks. — Manuals
I. Title
332.1'753'0941

Typeset in 10½/11pt, Times roman, by Kerrypress Ltd, Luton, Beds
Text printed on mf 80 gsm. Cover 240 gsm blade coated matt.
Printed and bound by Staples Printers Rochester Limited, Rochester, Kent.

CONTENTS

ACKNOWLEDGEMENTS

Firstly, I must thank the Directors of Barclays Bank plc for allowing me to bring the material of *Guide to Good Lending Practices* to a wider audience.

I am also greatly indebted to my colleagues, John Broadbent, David Burstow, Richard Carlson, George Cracknell, Eddie Creeden, Brian Grant, Duncan Homan, Ray James, Stanley Kemp, David Metcalfe, Alan Ruddle and Stanley Sutton, whose brains I picked when in doubt and who corrected me when I was wrong. Any remaining errors are mine not theirs.

Finally, I should like to express my appreciation to Geoffrey Sales, Consultant at The Chartered Institute of Bankers, and Tony Davies, Senior Manager, Royal Trust Bank, for their help in reviewing and adapting the material.

PREFACE

Since May 1988, I have been Chief Examiner for Practice of Banking 2. This examination has historically had a low pass rate—generally around 20%. I have now personally marked over 700 papers, a high proportion of them marginal failures, and it is clear to me that part of the reason for the low pass rate is that candidates with little direct experience of lending find it difficult to adopt the practical approach which is necessary to score well on the lending questions. This book has been written with the aim of giving such candidates an insight into the techniques which experienced lenders use in their credit analysis. It is based on the Barclays Bank internal lending manual, *Guide to Good Lending Practices*, which I wrote in late 1986 and early 1987.

My background is as an ordinary branch banker whose interest in formal training/education was, until relatively recently, solely as a recipient. Although I had always regarded myself as a good lender, it came as a surprise when, in 1986, I was asked to write *Guide to Good Lending Practices*. After the initial shock had worn off, it became apparent to me that there was a book to be written which would go beyond the largely theoretical approach to lending usually adopted in textbooks and on training courses.

Sound theoretical knowledge is obviously essential to a good lender. Experienced bankers often describe lending as being an art rather than a science because there are occasions when they do not always follow the theoretical rules but are able to justify a different way of dealing with a problem. The mixture of theory, experience and commonsense which good lenders apply produces better results than theory alone.

Is it possible to impart these extra ingredients of experience and commonsense in a book? There is no magic formula but the way forward in a proposition usually becomes clear if the lender thoroughly understands the risks involved. My aim has been to set out how risks arise in lending propositions and how they may be dealt with.

This book will not only be a textbook for examination candidates, but will also be a source of help to which lenders can turn to when they are in doubt on how to deal with difficult or unfamiliar propositions.

C N Rouse FCIB
February 1989

To Frank Schofield and David Burstow — two of the best teachers a young banker could have had

PART A

GENERAL PRINCIPLES OF LENDING

1 GENERAL PRINCIPLES OF LENDING

In this first chapter, the ground rules for lending will be established. Rules is perhaps not the right word because experienced lenders use a mixture of technical knowledge and common sense rather than rules.

Each lending case has to be treated on its merits, but there are a number of general principles which should be applied in all cases.

The content of this chapter will be dealt with under two headings:

(a) A Philosophy for Lending
(b) A Methodical Approach to Appraisal

(A) A PHILOSOPHY FOR LENDING

Art or Science?
A lender 'lends' money and does not give it away. There is a judgment therefore that at some future date repayment will take place. The lender needs to look into the future and ask, will the customer repay by the agreed date? There will always be some risk that the customer will be unable to repay, and it is in assessing this risk that the lender needs to demonstrate both skill and judgment.

The lender's objective will be to assess the extent of the risk and to try to reduce the amount of uncertainty that will exist over the prospect of repayment. Whilst there are guidelines to follow, there is no 'magic formula'. The lender must gather together all the relevant information and then apply his or her skills to making a judgment.

'Number crunching' will never be enough, and this is why many experienced lenders describe lending as an 'art' rather than a 'science'.

The Professional Approach
Lenders must seek to arrive at an objective decision. This is not as easy as it sounds as there will always be pressures from customers and elsewhere, for example the need to meet profit targets, which may sway the lender's judgment. A customer may press for a quick

answer when the lender does not feel there is adequate information. The approach of the true professional is to resist outside pressures and to insist on sufficient time and information to understand and evaluate the proposition. It is the lender who is taking the risk and it is not professional to reach the wrong decision.

The professional lender who is confident in his or her ability will always apply the following principles:

(i) Take time to reach a decision—detailed financial information takes time to be absorbed. If possible, it is preferable to get the 'paperwork' before the interview so that it can be assessed and any queries identified.

(ii) Not be too proud to ask for a second opinion—some of the smallest lending decisions can be the hardest.

(iii) Get full information from the customer and not make unnecessary assumptions or 'fill in' missing detail.

(iv) Not take a customer's statements at face value and ask for evidence which will provide independent corroboration.

(v) Distinguish between facts, estimates and opinions when forming a judgment.

(vi) Think again when the 'gut reaction' suggests caution even though the factual assessment looks satisfactory.

(B) A METHODICAL APPROACH TO APPRAISAL

There are five stages to any analysis of a new lending proposition:

1 Introduction of the customer
2 The application by the customer
3 Review of the application
4 Evaluation
5 Monitoring and control.

Introduction

Lenders do not have to do business with people they do not feel comfortable with. References are no longer taken on every occasion when an account is opened, but the account opening procedures should be such as to establish, as far as possible, that the customer is honest and trustworthy. This is especially important when the customer wishes to borrow at a later stage and, if there is any doubt, a reference should be insisted upon.

Approaches for borrowing from customers of other banks merit special caution. Why is the approach being made at all? Has the proposal already been rejected by the other bank? If the potential customer ought to have a financial track record but does not appear to have one, a degree of suspicion is in order.

An important source of new business for most lenders is introductions from professional advisers such as accountants and solicitors. This is not to say that a bank is obliged to lend to customers introduced in this way. Indeed, there is no evidence to suggest that such customers are generally of better quality than others. The bank should treat each case on its merits and subject each proposition to an objective assessment.

Some introducers try to put pressure on the lender by, for example, suggesting that further introductions may be dependent on agreement to a specific proposition. The lender must not succumb to such pressure and needs to avoid relying too heavily on any individual source of new business. A good introducer will respect a lender who shows objectivity, whilst caving in under pressure will only result in being considered a 'soft touch' and generate the introduction of other less attractive prospects.

The Application

This can take many forms but should include a plan for repaying the borrowing and an assessment of the contingencies which might reasonably arise and how the borrower would intend to deal with them.

It might be in detailed written form or merely verbal. There are many instances when the lender will have to draw out sufficient further information to enable the risks in the proposition to be fully assessed.

Review of the Application

At this stage all the relevant information which is required needs to be tested and other data sought if necessary. Either formally or informally the lender applies what are generally known as the canons of good lending. The main areas common to all lending propositions are examined in some detail.

It is sometimes difficult to remember all the points to be covered during an interview and many lenders use a mnemonic as a check list. There are a number of mnemonics in common use, but the most common are probably CCCPARTS (Character, Capital, Capability, Purpose, Amount, Repayment, Terms, Security), PARSER (Person, Amount, Repayment, Security, Expediency, Remuneration) and CAMPARI. CAMPARI which is used by two of the major clearing banks, is probably the most popular of the mnemonics and is the one described in detail here. It stands for:

Character
Ability
Margin
Purpose
Amount
Repayment
Insurance (Security)

Character
Although some might claim otherwise, it is virtually impossible to assess an individual's character after just one meeting. It is an extremely difficult area but a vital one to get right. Facts, not opinion are crucial, e.g.:

— How reliable is the customer's word as regards the details of the proposition and the promise of repayment?
— Does the customer make exaggerated claims which are far too optimistic or is a more modest and reasonable approach adopted?
— Is the customer's track record good? Was there any previous borrowing, and if so, was it repaid without trouble?
— If the customer is new, why are we being approached? Can bank statements be seen to assess the conduct of the account?

Ability
This aspect relates to the borrower's ability in managing financial affairs and is similar to character as far as personal customers are concerned.
   Further points in respect of business customers would include:

— Is there a good spread of skill and experience among the management team in, for example, production, marketing and finance?
— Does the management team hold relevant professional qualifications?
— Are they committed to making the company successful?
— Where the finance is earmarked for a specific area of activity, do they have the necessary experience in that area?

Margin
Agreement should be reached at the outset with the borrower in respect of interest margin, commission and other relevant fees. The interest margin will be a reflection of the risk involved in the lending,

whilst commission and other fees will be determined by the amount and complexity of the work involved.

It should never be forgotten that banks are in business to make profits and to give shareholders a fair return on their capital.

Purpose

The lender will want to verify that the purpose is acceptable.

Perhaps the facility would not be in the customer's best interests. Customers do tend to overlook problems in their optimism and, if the bank can bring a degree of realism to the proposition at the outset, it may be more beneficial to the customer than agreeing to the requested advance.

Amount

Is the customer asking for either too much or too little? There are dangers in both and it is important therefore to establish that the amount requested is correct and that all incidental expenses have been considered. The good borrower will have allowed for contingencies.

The amount requested should be in proportion to the customer's own resources and contribution. A reasonable contribution from the borrower shows commitment and a buffer is provided by the customer's stake should problems arise.

Repayment

The real risk in lending is to be found in the assessment of the repayment proposals. It is important that the source of repayment is made clear from the outset and the lender must establish the degree of certainty that the promised funds will be received.

Where the source of repayment is income/cashflow, the lender will need projections to ensure that there are surplus funds to cover repayment after meeting other commitments.

Insurance/Security

Ideally, the canons of lending should be satisfied irrespective of available security, but security is often considered necessary in case the repayment proposals fail to materialise.

It is vital that the provider of security, especially third party security, understands fully the consequences of charging it to the bank. It is equally important that no advance is made until security procedures have been completed, or are at least at a stage where completion can take place without the need to involve the borrower any further.

Evaluation

Once the available information has been assembled, an evaluation of the proposition can be made. This should be done in two stages:

1 An assessment of the feasibility of the borrower's plan for repayment. If the proposal is not viable, it is pointless to continue.
2 A critical appraisal of what might realistically go wrong—the likelihood of such events occurring and the effect on the bank's position.

The aim of this evaluation is to establish the risk involved. Listing the pros and cons of a proposition is often helpful. More reliance should be placed on facts and evidence than on estimates and opinions.

Once the lending has been made, the risk lies in the way the customer handles any problems which might arise. The lender's evaluation should concentrate on understanding the borrower's risks and assessing the ability of the borrower to deal with them.

The realisation of security may provide a source of repayment in the last resort. However the sale of security is rarely as straight forward in practice as it appears in theory and security valuations often do not stand up to the ultimate test of realisation.

There will be many cases where the lender feels the risk in a proposition is not tenable. A lender will wish to help a good customer and, if a proposition can be 're-engineered' into a more acceptable form, this should be done.

Monitoring and Control

It is highly unlikely that a customer's expectations will go exactly to plan and it is necessary for the lender to review progress regularly. The earlier that problems can be identified, the better will be the chances of controlling them and of providing practical advice to the customer, which in turn will protect the lender's position.

Regular monitoring of corporate accounts can also enhance the lender's image in the eyes of the customer. It provides evidence to the customer of a wish to understand the underlying business and to be involved in helping solve future problems.

A plan for monitoring should be established at the beginning and, where the provision of regular information from the customer is necessary, suitable arrangements should be made and followed up.

PART B

PERSONAL LENDING

2 SMALL PERSONAL LENDING

In the distant past relatively few people had bank accounts and all personal lending could be dealt with on an individual basis, with each proposition being assessed separately. The growth in the number of people with bank accounts has meant that over recent years banks have found it more cost effective to move to a 'systems' basis for most personal lending, with the adoption of Credit Scoring techniques and the wide-spread use of unadvised overdraft limits.

In general the systems approach works well but there will always be instances, for example, where a customer exceeds an unadvised limit, when individual appraisal will be necessary. In such cases, the canons of good lending and the approach suggested in the previous chapter should be applied to enable a satisfactory decision to be reached.

This chapter describes the different types of personal lending available and the assumptions behind the main forms of lending system currently used by banks. There are obviously differences between the types of system in use in banks so it is only possible to discuss them in general terms.

APPRAISING THE PROPOSITION

Some of the smallest lending decisions can be the hardest to make. There is often inadequate information available when a junior official has to decide whether or not to pay a large cheque for a personal customer. A large measure of commonsense has to be applied and inexperienced lenders would be well advised to seek advice from more senior staff when in doubt.

Since 1985 the full provisions of the Consumer Credit Act 1974 have come into effect. The requirements of this Act should always be considered—if only to be dismissed as inapplicable in the instance under review—as failure to follow the regulations or to complete the correct documentation may make a lending technically irrecoverable. All banks have their own manuals and forms covering the Consumer Credit Act requirements and there is insufficient space here to give this important consideration in personal lending any more than a passing acknowledgement.

OVERDRAFTS

Overdrafts are provided to cover borrowing of a temporary fluctuating nature which will be repaid on the receipt of expected funds. If a borrowing request does not conform to this definition, then the facility would be best provided in the form of a loan.

Overdrafts can be split into two categories:

1   Agreed overdrafts.
2   Unauthorised overdrafts.

1   Agreed Overdrafts

Agreed overdraft limits fall into two types:

(a) Short-term—to cover a specific requirement. Essentially a small bridging facility and the source and timing of the repayment should be made clear at the outset.

Consideration should be given to obtaining control over the source of repayment by, for example, selling shares which are to be the source of repayment through the bank's own broker.

Such facilities will usually be 'one offs' with individual appraisal being necessary.

(b) Renewable/revolving—a facility which is essentially to be used as a standby.

Into this category fall Save & Borrow Accounts and Budget Accounts as well as ordinary overdraft facilities. Assessment may be by way of Credit Scoring or individual appraisal. With the latter it will be necessary for the lender to be satisfied that a customer's future income will be sufficient to repay any temporary borrowing.

For higher income earners, Gold Card overdraft facilities of around £10,000 will be available on an unsecured basis. Such facilities will be granted subject to annual review and should not be allowed to provide solid permanent borrowing. High income earners may be tempted to arrange such facilities with a number of banks so that the degree of control a lender will have may be undermined. It is prudent to insist that a reasonable level of turnover is put through the account and a full fluctuation on a regular basis seen if significant use of the facility is made. There is clearly a danger in allowing a hardcore facility to be renewed over and over again simply because a customer meets a specified income level.

2   Unauthorised Overdrafts

For most customers there is a level to which a bank would be prepared to allow an overdraft without insisting on a formal arrangement. It is not cost effective or realistic in these days of readily available consumer credit to require that a customer always asks before going overdrawn.

Banks generally have coped with this problem by setting an overdraft limit on individual accounts which has not been advised to the customer. These limits have usually been related to a percentage of the customer's monthly salary—generally between 30% and 50%—with the borrowing expected to be taken only within say 10 days of normal receipt of salary. Customers are enabled to meet mortgage repayments and other monthly commitments prior to receiving their salaries without a large number of decisions having to be taken by the bank as to whether or not to pay individual cheques, standing orders or direct debits.

For an unadvised limit system to be effective in day to day use, it is important that there is general confidence amongst lending staff that individual limits have been set at the correct level. Although the percentage of salary method is a good rough guide, the essential point about marking individual limits is that the limit should represent the point to which the lender would be prepared to pay an account before taking some sort of positive action. There is no point marking a limit which, when exceeded, results in no action being taken— in such an instance the limit should be higher if the system is to achieve the maximum benefits in terms of cost effectiveness. Thus when an unadvised limit is exceeded, the borrower should at least be advised of the position on the account either by a statement or letter. In extreme cases it may be necessary to dishonour cheques.

The appearance of an excess over an unadvised limit more than 10 days in advance of the salary receipt could indicate impending problems and any excess over an unadvised limit should lead to a review of the account to ensure that the assumptions on which the original limit was marked have not changed.

PERSONAL LOANS

Most lenders now assess personal loans through a mixture of Credit Scoring and the use of Credit Reference Agencies.

Credit Scoring is a different kind of lending technique to that described in Chapter 1. It is essentially a statistical method of assessment which works by picking out characteristics which, based on the lender's experience, are likely to apply to a suitable applicant. Each piece of information on the application form is given a score;

if the total of these scores is above a set 'passmark', the loan would probably be approved.

If the score falls in the grey area around the passmark or, in the case of some institutions, on all occasions, a lender may check with a Credit Reference Agency. These agencies hold basic details on around 40 million people, name and address, type and terms of credit agreements, bad debts, County Court judgments, etc. Most agencies record against addresses rather than individuals and the Data Protection Act requires that information be kept for a reasonable time only, so the information given needs to be subjected to a degree of commonsense interpretation.

Traditional lenders often treat Credit Scoring with a degree of suspicion and may sometimes be tempted to override a Credit Scoring decision when they feel that the answer given is wrong. Credit Scoring gives an entirely objective decision. To give an outrageous—and incorrect—example: if 100% of people with red hair always repay their loans, then the characteristic of having red hair will be given a high score in a Credit Scoring system. Credit Scoring is based wholly on statistical probabilities in relation to individual characteristics. A traditional lender will form a subjective view of an applicant and the overriding of a Credit Scoring decision not based on statistics will distort the information base. As the passmark in the system will be set and varied in relation to the performance of the statistical information, constant overriding will damage the information base and undermine the system's effective operation.

This need to maintain a sound statistical base means that Credit Scored Personal Loans should not be used for 'rescue operations' or the rescheduling of debts to reduce a customer's unsupportable monthly commitments. The inclusion of such lending, which by definition carries a higher than normal risk, would be likely to distort the true bad debt performance of the system and such arrangements should only be dealt with outside the system, usually by a Base Rate Linked Loan.

BASE RATE LINKED LOANS

These will usually (although not always) be a cheaper form of borrowing than the standard bank personal loan. Banks will therefore prefer to lend by way of a personal loan but there will be occasions when a base rate linked loan might be appropriate for certain customers. The main examples will be:

(a) where the amount is in excess of the personal loan limit or the purpose does not qualify;
(b) where equal monthly repayments are not appropriate;

(c) where security is considered necessary;
(d) rescheduling of borrowing;
(e) for high value customers where competitive pressures indicate a finer interest rate, for example, customers who would qualify for a Gold Card.

Individual assessment of such loans will be necessary using the canons of lending and approach set out in Chapter 1.

Loans granted for the rescheduling of borrowing need to be examined with particular care. A previous promise of repayment has usually proved to be too optimistic and, by definition, the customer's track record leaves something to be desired. The risk must be higher than normal and such arrangements should only usually be undertaken if a good potential alternative form of repayment is available in the form of acceptable security.

MONITORING AND CONTROL

Reasons for Monitoring Accounts

Monitoring is the boring part of lending and is often given a low priority by less than conscientious lenders. Accounts need to be monitored for the following reasons:

(a) to be fully aware of the up to date situation on an account to ensure any borrowing which has been granted remains within the customer's capacity to repay;
(b) to observe any adverse trends so that early action can be taken, for example, increasing or earlier anticipation of salary;
(c) to discover any irregular practices—the banks have recently been criticised for allowing the proceeds of crime to be 'laundered' through accounts without sufficient enquiry;
(d) to be informed about a customer's activities and credit worthiness, for example, evidence of gambling;
(e) to ensure that the customer is using the advance for the agreed purpose;
(f) to confirm information provided by the customer, for example, amount of salary and monthly commitments.

Methods of Monitoring

It is unrealistic to seek to monitor every personal customer in a bank branch. The need is to be selective and concentrate efforts on those accounts which are likely to give cause for concern. The proper use of unadvised limits will reduce the number of accounts which have to be kept under constant review—although the size of all unadvised limits needs to be reassessed at least annually. Bank branches have a large amount of information available to them for monitoring purposes. This information can be categorised into three main types:

1   Computer printouts
2   Customer statement sheets
3   Entry vouchers.

1   Computer Printouts

Different banks have different computer systems and produce different printouts. However all of them have the capacity to supply historical information on the trend on individual customer accounts. When looking at this information the main questions which should be asked are:

(a)   What is the worst balance trend? Are there excesses over the limit?
(b)   What is the best balance trend? Is there any evidence of a hardcore developing?
(c)   Is the average balance figure worsening?
(d)   Is the turnover through the account out of line with what might have been expected?
(e)   Has there been a change in the run of the account compared to previous years?

An adverse trend in just one of these need not be a cause for concern, but when a deterioration is evident in more than one, then some action may be necessary, even if this is limited to keeping the account under more regular review.

2   Customer Statement Sheets

Customer statement information tends to be standard among the banks. The information produced is to give the customer an account of individual debits and credits and is not therefore in an ideal form for bank monitoring purposes. Specifically produced computer printouts will be more 'user friendly' but when a more detailed review of an account is needed, an examination of statements can be very revealing.

The questions which an examination of statements may help answer include:

(a)   Is there any pressure on an overdraft limit or is the account working satisfactorily and showing healthy fluctuations?

(b) Does the balance give a true picture or has it been distorted by unusual/exceptional items?
(c) Is turnover through the account rising sharply? This might be evidence of crossfiring.
(d) When are credits received? Is the monthly salary still being received regularly?
(e) To whom are any regular payments out of the account made?
(f) Is there any change in the character of the account?
(g) Are there any unusual items passing through the account?

3 Entry Vouchers

The examination of all debits and credits through a customer's account will be very time consuming and needs to be especially selective. Effort should therefore be concentrated on:

(a) those accounts which require special attention;
(b) entries for larger amounts.

An examination of debit entries will show:

(a) Evidence of a customer's interests and financial activities, for example:
borrowing—payments to HP or other finance companies;
gambling—cheques to bookmakers;
associates—membership fees to clubs or payment to a church or charitable institutions;
thrift—regular payments to saving institutions and insurance companies.
(b) Whether the borrowing is being used for the purpose for which it was agreed. This may not represent a problem but it does give evidence of a customer's truthfulness and might be a cause for concern.

An examination of credit will show:

(a) the source of a customer's income—salary, dividends, etc.;
(b) whether uncleared effects are possibly going to be a problem;
(c) suspicious transactions—can large cash receipts be explained?

Methods of Control

The process of controlling a borrowing can be split into two elements:

1 Review
2 Action

1 Review

The most common form of lending decision is that which involves the payment of a cheque or other debit where no overdraft limit exists or the limit which is marked is being exceeded. The major banks have daily computer printouts which identify such cheques and debits on a daily basis. Items which are to be returned need to be dealt with before noon so the period available for decision is limited. A quick review of the account has to be carried out using the monitoring information mentioned in the previous section and applying the canons of lending set out in Chapter 1.

The review of other types of personal lending can be a measured process, with time available for discussion with the customer and the ability to call for more information if necessary.

Having reached a decision, it is useful to make some sort of brief note which can be quickly referred to in future to avoid duplication of effort in any subsequent review.

2 Action

After the review has taken place some sort of action will have to be taken if only a decision to do nothing.

The courses of action available to a lender when things go seriously wrong with a borrowing are set out in Chapter 5, so the examination of what to do will be limited here to considerations surrounding the payment of cheques and other debits.

The first decision which needs to be reached over the item is whether to pay it or not. The canons of lending should be applied. If the decision is to pay, then consideration needs to be given as to whether a customer ought to be advised formally of the situation on the account so that action can be taken to restore it to credit or within the limit. For most customers it will not be possible to rectify the position until the next wages or salary credit is received. By looking at the account some sort of judgment should be possible as to how much higher the overdraft might go in order that some sort of warning may be issued to the customer.

A decision not to pay will require that the cheque or other debit be returned.

Return of Cheques

The return of a cheque is a serious matter for a customer and the decision should not be taken lightly. A number of checks should be made before a cheque is returned and these are:

(a) that no credit has been received since the balance report showing the unacceptable overdraft;

(b) the customer's statement sheet and paid vouchers should be examined to ensure that there have been no mis-posts and that no postdated cheques have been paid recently;

(c) accounts in similar names should be examined to ensure that credits have not been placed on the wrong account;

(d) that there are no funds on a savings account in the same name;

(e) no overdraft or loan facility has recently been agreed which would cover the borrowing;

(f) the cheque has not been guaranteed by a cheque card or paid under an open credit arrangement;

(g) whether funds are due, for example, from the sale of shares;

(h) whether there are items held in safe custody, for example, shares, which might be sold to clear the borrowing;

(i) has the account been paid higher than the present figure previously without a warning to the customer?

(j) if this is the first occasion a cheque is to be returned, has an attempt been made to contact the customer to find out what has gone wrong?

Once a decision has been taken to return a cheque, consideration should also be given to cancelling all standing orders, direct debit mandates and, in extreme cases, giving notice to close the account. Customers for whom cheques have regularly to be returned are not worth having.

3 LARGE PERSONAL LENDING

This chapter deals with the larger kind of borrowing proposition with which a lender can be faced. It also covers certain other types of lending where businesses are not involved and individual liability plays a major role.

Subject matter will be covered under the following headings:

(a) Home Loans
(b) Bridging Loans
(c) Lending to Executors and Administrators
(d) Lending to Trustees
(e) Lending to Clubs and Associations

(A) HOME LOANS

Appraising New Propositions
The canons of good lending and the approach set out in Chapter 1 should be applied to each proposition.

Character/Ability

The borrower ought to have a track record with the bank or, if not, evidence should be seen of the track record with his or her present bankers in the form of bank statements. The home loan business is very competitive and this is one area where there is less need to be sceptical if a potential borrower is switching banks to obtain the best deal.

The borrower should be in employment which will supply a stable income. The career prospects of the applicant may be important as future income earning potential may have a bearing on marginal decisions.

Margin

The interest rate will be the lender's current mortgage rate. If possible a suitable fee for arranging the facility should be obtained, but competitive pressures are making this increasingly difficult.

The costs of establishing the facility should be recouped, including such elements as valuation fees.

There will be an opportunity to earn other income from selling other products such as mortgage protection and fire insurance.

All in all this can be a very remunerative form of lending.

Purpose

The purchase of a house for owner occupation will almost always be acceptable to a lender. More problematical will be loans requested for the purchase of second and holiday homes or where owner occupation is not going to take place immediately and a period of letting is envisaged, for example, where the borrower is going to spend a period abroad. Different lenders will have different policies for dealing with such situations.

Concern is sometimes expressed about lenders using short term deposits to fund long term liabilities like home loans. It needs to be recognised that the average life of a home loan is only seven years so that *on average*, the true term is likely to be much shorter than the commitment is given for.

Amount

The amount borrowed should be sufficient to cover all the costs of purchase including legal fees and the costs of any essential repairs indicated as being necessary in the valuer's report. It may be wise not to advance the cost of repairs/improvements until there is independent evidence that they have been completed.

Repayment

Different institutions will allow different terms for home loans. The usual term will be 25 years, although some lenders may be prepared to go to 35 years.

A typical guideline for assessing repayment capacity is three times the gross main income plus once any secondary income, but the overriding consideration is the ability of the applicant to comfortably service the borrowing. For example, a single man will be able to afford to repay much more easily than a married family man with a similar level of income.

Mortgage rates can rise very rapidly during a year and too much emphasis should not be placed on the ability to service borrowing at whatever the current rate is. It is prudent to consider if the borrower could still service the loan if rates rose by, say, 2%, particularly if interest rates look to be at an historical low point.

Evidence of income should be seen in the form of either bank statements or some other independent proof.

If repayment looks marginal, the borrower should be asked to provide a personal budget showing his income and expenditure on the assumption that the property has been purchased. An assessment can then be made as to whether repayment remains viable after allowing for increased expenditure on rates, lighting, heating, etc.

Insurance/Security

The prime security will be a first mortgage over the property being purchased. There is an increasing trend in the purchase of property abroad, but the complications of taking foreign security are great, and most lenders will insist that the property be in the United Kingdom.

If a property is leasehold, most lenders will insist that the lease has at least 60 years to run.

If new building is involved the lending should be made against architects' certificates or subject to the standard NHBC agreement.

A first mortgage will also be required over sufficient life cover to ensure that the loan is repaid on the death of the applicant, and acceptable property insurance which should be comprehensive and index linked for a sum not less than that recommended in the professional mortgage valuation. The property insurance should be in force from the date of exchange of contracts.

Monitoring and Control

Home loans need to be subjected to an annual review to ensure that the borrowing is reducing according to plan where repayment loans are concerned, and all commitments are being met where endowment facilities have been granted.

Problems in servicing the borrowing will be reflected first in the conduct of the borrower's current account. For this reason the lender will ideally wish to maintain the borrower's main banking account. When difficulty in meeting payments becomes evident, the borrower will need to be interviewed without delay. Provided the problem appears to be a temporary one, some restructuring of the repayment programme may be possible. But if there appears to be a permanent difficulty, then the borrower needs to be encouraged to recognise this and face the necessity of selling the property before mounting interest eats into the equity.

(B) BRIDGING LOANS

This section will cover bridging loans for house purchase, although the term can be applied to any loan, which is used to purchase an asset, where repayment is to come from the sale of a different asset, or from the receipt of funds from a known source.

There are two main types of bridging loan: closed and open-ended. With both types, loans can be for the full purchase price of the property or for the deposit required when contracts are exchanged, usually 10%.

Calculating the Amount

Most lenders will have an aide-memoire or form which can be completed when interviewing the borrower to ensure that no relevant points are omitted and that the amount is correctly calculated.

The calculation of the amount is best illustrated by an example in which legal fees, etc., have been omitted for the sake of clarity:

| Selling | £51,000 | Outstanding Mortgage | £25,000 |
| Buying | £67,000 | New Mortgage | £45,000 |

If the 10% deposit only is required, the limit will be £6,700 and this will be repaid:

	£
Equity in present property	26,000
Plus new mortgage	45,000
	71,000
Less balance of purchase price	60,300
Surplus available for repayment	10,700

When the borrower requires full funding of the purchase, there are usually two alternatives:

1   Advancing the full purchase price. The limit will be £67,000, to be repaid from the equity in the present property of £26,000, and the new mortgage of £45,000.
2   Clearing the existing mortgage to allow drawdown of the new mortgage, and advancing the balance of the purchase price.

The limit will then be:

	£
Purchase price	67,000
Less new mortgage	45,000
	22,000
Plus, to clear present mortgage	25,000
	47,000

The loan will be repaid by the sale proceeds of the existing property, i.e. £51,000.

The second alternative will be available only:

(a)   when the new mortgage is greater than the old;
(b)   when the new mortgage is available on completion of the purchase.

Expenses

Expenses were excluded from the previous examples, but they usually come to a significant sum in this type of transaction and have to be allowed for in the calculations.

It is impossible to give definite figures for costs involved in property purchase and sale, and it should be remembered that the figures shown below are only a guideline. They will also be prone to go out of date as the business of conveying property becomes more competitive or there are changes in taxation levels. At the time of writing, however, it does seem likely that any changes will have the effect of reducing costs so that the figures below may be considered as conservative.

Property Transactions—Purchase

Consideration £	Legal Fees etc. £	Stamp Duty £	Total £
30,000	250	NIL	250
40,000	300	400	700
50,000	350	500	850
60,000	400	600	1,000
80,000	500	800	1,300
100,000	600	1,000	1,600

Property Transactions—Sale

Consideration £	Legal Fees etc. £	Estate Agent's Fee (2% + VAT) £	Total £
30,000	200	690	890
40,000	250	920	1,170
50,000	300	1,150	1,450
60,000	350	1,380	1,730
80,000	450	1,840	2,290
100,000	550	2,300	2,850

The following points should also be borne in mind:

(a) All transactions are different, and solicitors' fees in particular will vary according to the complexity as well as the amount of the transaction.
(b) There may be considerable variations in what estate agents and solicitors will charge, even in the same town.
(c) Where registered land is involved, Land Registry charges will increase the total costs.
(d) The complexity of examination of title will increase the costs where the conveyance of unregistered land is concerned.
(e) The interest charges and other fees of the lender also need to be taken into account.

The Risks in Closed Bridging Loans

A closed bridge is one where contracts have been exchanged, with a firm completion date with respect to the sale of the existing property, which represents the source of repayment. Since such contracts are legally binding, the lending risks are low provided a solicitor's undertaking is obtained to ensure sale proceeds are received. Exchange of contracts does not, however, guarantee that a sale will take place, and problems can still arise in the following circumstances:

(a) The buyer does not have the finance to complete the purchase. A reputable solicitor would never allow contracts to be exchanged if the necessary resources to complete were not available, but it can happen. Close liaison with the solicitor will be essential, although this will have to take place indirectly through the buyer's solicitor. It is becoming increasingly common for deposits less than 10% to be paid, but if a deposit below, say, 5% is offered, then particular caution may be appropriate.
(b) Completion being conditional. For example, the buyer might have an option to withdraw from the purchase of a property being built or improved if building work is not finished on time. Alternatively, completion may be dependent on the buyer having a mortgage available.
(c) Fixtures and fittings forming a significant part of the purchase or sale price as these will not form part of the lender's security if things go wrong. A full professional valuation of the properties should avoid this, but such valuations are not always taken in bridging loan situations, particularly if the bridge appears to be closed.
(d) Collusion between buyer and seller, who might mutually agree not to go ahead with the transaction. There is nothing the lender

can do to ensure that the transaction goes ahead in such circumstances, and care should be taken when it is known that the buyer and seller are acquainted.

The safest course of action to take when there is doubt that completion will occur as planned is to treat the facility as an open-ended bridge.

The Risks in Open-Ended Bridging Loans

Although the United Kingdom housing market has generally shown a steady upward trend, there have been periods when the market has been very flat. Repayment of open-ended bridging loans is significantly affected by market conditions, and a borrower can be caught out and repayment of the loan become protracted.

Requests for open-ended bridges often arise in circumstances where the borrower may not be taking an entirely objective view of the risks involved, e.g. a unique opportunity to buy the particular house. The risks must be explained, especially as entering into an open-ended commitment can involve a borrower in a 'squeeze' from both ends of the transaction if it is long drawn out. This is because:

(a) interest accrues extremely quickly, e.g. a £50,000 loan at 14% will account for £3,500 of the customer's money in only six months;

(b) failure to obtain an early sale together with the rapid build up in interest costs will pressurise the borrower into reducing the asking price for the existing property.

A lender would be wise not to consider an open-ended bridging loan unless:

(a) the housing market is buoyant and looks like staying so in the immediate future;

(b) an early sale of the existing property is in prospect, i.e. a definite buyer has been found;

(c) there is a substantial margin to cover all contingencies—the anticipated net sale proceeds should repay the loan plus twelve months accrued interest, and at the same time allow for a 20% reduction in the asking price.

In the previous example of a £50,000 loan at 14% the net proceeds would have to be at least £71,250 in order to provide a sufficient margin (£50,000 loan plus accrued interest of £7,000 × $^5/_4$ = £71,250).

If additional good liquid security, for example, stocks and shares, is available, this can be used to add to the margin in the transaction but it should be charged at the outset.

General Considerations

(a) The provisions of the Consumer Credit Act should be taken into account but it should be recognised that it is the total amount to be advanced which is the deciding factor as to whether a loan is regulated, not the amount of any individual tranche.

(b) Advances for property purchase must be made on loan account in order for any tax benefits to be claimed.

(c) Where the deposit only is being advanced, it will still be necessary to assess the complete transaction in case problems arise and the borrower makes an approach for further funds. It would not be wise to lend for the deposit unless the lender was prepared to lend the full amount if necessary.

(d) Written confirmation should be obtained from the borrower's solicitor that contracts for both sale and purchase have been exchanged.

(e) Solicitor's undertakings should be obtained in respect of monies due and/or deeds to come. Consideration needs to be given to taking formal charges over the properties and this will be particularly appropriate if the bridge is open-ended.

(f) Where the source of repayment is a mortgage from another lender, confirmation will be required of the amount and when it is due, together with an undertaking to send the monies. If part of the borrower's own contribution to the transaction is to come from some other source, similar considerations will also apply.

(g) If the loan is being provided to enable a property to be built, the lender should ensure:

    (i) the builders are reliable;

    (ii) the contract is either fixed price or on reasonable terms;

    (iii) advances are made only against architects' certificates at pre-determined stages of development;

    (iv) an NHBC certificate will be available if the ultimate mortgage lender will require this.

(h) Realistic valuations have been placed on the properties. This will be particularly important with open-ended bridging loans where the lender needs to be sure that both properties are worth the asking price. Where the margin is tight, professional valuations should be considered.

(i) Full insurance cover is essential as soon as contracts are exchanged.
(j) Status enquiries will be necessary on solicitors who are not known. Mortgage fraud is on the increase and this is not an area in which corners should be cut.

(C) LENDING TO EXECUTORS AND ADMINISTRATORS

There are three main categories into which advances to personal representatives will fall:

1 Lending prior to the grant of probate or administration to enable settlement of the debts of the estate.
2 Lending for payment of inheritance tax so that probate or grant of administration can be obtained.
3 Lending after probate or grant of administration, usually to allow the beneficial winding up of the estate.

Whilst personal representatives are personally liable for any borrowing, they incur only joint liability unless their agreement to joint and several liability is obtained.

Personal representatives are only 'prospective' before probate or administration is granted, and therefore any lending is entirely against their personal liability. Charges given by executors over estate assets before probate become effective only after it is granted, whilst charges cannot be executed by administrators until after grant of administration.

Security previously charged by the deceased is not available for advances to personal representatives, unless they recharge it.

Whilst an unsecured lender will be relying solely on the personal liability of representatives, they have the right to be indemnified out of the estate and the lender will be subrogated to their position for any lending.

Of the three categories mentioned above, the most common form of advance is for payment of inheritance tax in order to obtain probate or administration. Such advances will normally be agreed, provided the lender can be satisfied:

(a) in respect of the integrity of the personal representatives and their solicitor;
(b) that the amount of inheritance tax payable is reasonable;
(c) that the advance can be repaid quickly from the realisation of liquid assets.

(D)   LENDING TO TRUSTEES

As with executors and administrators, trustees are personally liable for any borrowing, but only jointly unless agreement to joint and several liability is obtained. The lender would need to be satisfied with the financial standing of the trustees before lending against their undertaking to repay. Alternatively, or additionally, the trustees might be requested to offer adequate security to cover their personal liability.

Although trustees have no implied power to charge trust assets, they will be able to so:

(a)   When authorised to do so under the terms of the trust.
(b)   Under the Trustee Act 1925, s. 16, when, by the terms of the trust, or by statute, the trustees have power to pay or apply capital money for any specific purpose, and the charge is to secure monies raised for that purpose.
(c)   Under the Settled Land Act 1925, s. 71, where trustees for sale have similar powers to a tenant for life, in that they may borrow on mortgage for certain purposes (e.g. to pay off a charge on the property or to effect an improvement authorised by the trust, or by statute).
(d)   When trustees with no original power to charge trust property are authorised to do so by the beneficiaries.

Advances to trustees should be made on loan account when secured by trust property, but can be by way of overdraft when granted against the personal liability of the trustees.

(E)   LENDING TO CLUBS AND ASSOCIATIONS

Clubs and associations are not normally separate legal entities, nor do they have contractual powers, nor can they be sued for their debts.

Individual members are not personally liable for any debts undertaken by the officers, and despite there being legal precedent to indicate that committee members would be personally liable, the position is by no means certain.

The lender must ensure that somebody with the capacity to repay assumes full liability. The advance can then be made either on a separate account in the names of the responsible officers or in the name of the club supported by guarantees from the officers.

The borrowing must conform with any formalities and restrictions laid down in the rules, which will need to be checked for this purpose.

Since it is not permissible for a club or association to own property, it will be held in the names of trustees. The considerations mentioned in the previous section will apply in respect of charging trust property.

4 PERSONAL LENDING AND SECURITY

This chapter concentrates on the value of security taken to cover personal lending and the problems associated with it. It is not intended to deal with the technicalities of charging security which are well covered in other books. Security will be examined under the following headings:

(a) When should security be taken?
(b) Security margins.
(c) Property valuation.
(d) Second mortgages.
(e) Guarantees and other third party security.

(A) WHEN SHOULD SECURITY BE TAKEN?

A lender should consider taking security in the following situations:

(i) where the realisation of specific assets represents the source of repayment, e.g. a bridging loan;
(ii) where the purpose of the advance is to acquire a specific asset, e.g. a home loan;
(iii) where the risks and consequences of the expected source of repayment failing are such as to make it necessary to have a clearly defined and controlled alternative source.

The circumstances in which the first two situations will arise are obvious. Most difficulties will be found in assessing the third and it is this area which will be considered in detail. The evaluation can be split into two parts:

1 The risks—the likelihood of the expected source of repayment breaking down.
2 The consequences—if the primary source of repayment did fail,

would the lender obtain clearance of the borrowing if control over, and the power to sell, specific assets was not held?

A practical approach is needed and the lender should be 'amount conscious'. It will not be cost effective to take security for small sums, nor should items be charged which are difficult to control, value or realise (e.g. jewellery, antiques, etc.).

The primary source of repayment where personal borrowers in stable employment are concerned will usually be their income, although care will need to be exercised where a significant proportion of earnings is represented by overtime or commission.

Risks

The assessment of the possibility of repayment failure will be determined by:

(a) The margin between income and commitments—how comfortably can repayment be achieved from disposable income?
(b) The possibilities of major changes in personal circumstances, e.g. death, sickness, divorce, redundancy, etc. Can some of these risks be reduced by insurance?
(c) The term of the lending—the risk of adverse changes is greater over a long term rather than a short one.

Consequences

Whilst the risks are a product of the borrower's income and expenditure, when considering consequences it is his or her assets and liabilities which become important. In the absence of an income it is the surplus of assets over liabilities (including contingent liabilities) which will provide repayment.

The points to consider are:

(a) The size of the surplus in relation to the borrowing—a good margin is required. Valuation of assets should be on a forced sale basis, and account needs to be taken of any element of joint ownership, for example, a matrimonial home will not just belong to one party.
(b) The ease and speed with which assets can be realised. An asset portfolio containing a high proportion of quoted shares is preferable to one made up principally of the matrimonial home.
(c) The borrower's likely attitude in adversity—will assets be disposed of willingly to satisfy debts?

In those situations where the possibilities of repayment failure are significant and obtaining repayment from any alternative source looks difficult, serious consideration must be given to not lending at all. If it is decided to go ahead and lend, it would be wise to do so only on a secured basis.

(B)   SECURITY MARGINS

The most common forms of tangible security taken for personal lending are:

(a)   Land and property
(b)   Life policies
(c)   Stocks and shares

Why is a Margin Needed?

If a lending of 100% of security valuation is made, the realisation proceeds from the sale of the assets will not repay the full borrowing because they will not cover:

(a)   Any fall in value between the date of the advance and the sale of the asset. So with a long term lending, the uncertainty of realisable value may be greater and therefore a wider margin may be needed.
(b)   The costs of sale and other necessary costs relating to the need to keep the asset saleable, such as security, insurance and maintenance costs on a property.
(c)   The roll up of interest since the last charging date.

For a lender to be fully secured, the security margin should include a reasonable estimate of the effect of these elements on the security value. The absence of an adequate margin means that the advance may not be fully repaid from the sale of the security and it needs to be recognised that such a lending is, in reality, only partially secured, even though the face value of the security is greater than the lending.

Land and Property

Most professional property valuations are based on an open market value at the time of the valuation. This assumes a willing buyer and seller, and a reasonable period for the sale to be negotiated taking into account the nature of the property and the state of the market. Estimates of selling and legal fees can easily be obtained from local estate agents and solicitors, whilst 12 months would be a prudent assumption in respect of interest roll up, given that the period to be covered will begin when repayments stop—not when the property is put on the market. The main problem with the property will lie in translating its present open market value into a future forced sale value. This will be a subjective judgment influenced by the type, location, age, quality and condition of the property.

Where owner occupied residential property is concerned, experience has shown that a 20% security margin is about right. That is not to say that lenders do not advance more than 80% of the value of such properties but when they do so it is usually in conjunction with the provision of mortgage indemnity insurance to cover the gap.

Life Policies

The surrender values of life policies issued by reputable insurance companies provide stable security. There have been occasions where individual company surrender values have fallen, but these have been very rare and for practical purposes it can be assumed that a surrender value represents an accurate realisation value. It is wise to ensure that premiums are paid up to date as insurance companies can set off unpaid premiums against surrender values.

Realisation costs will be negligible, so the security margin needs only to cover potential interest roll up. On the assumption that a policy can be surrendered within one month and that the maximum period for which interest previously would have been unpaid would have been three months, a lending of 95% of surrender value should be fully covered by the security.

Stocks and Shares

Not all stocks and shares represent good security. Generally speaking, only quoted shares should be taken as security because unquoted shares, particularly those in private companies, are difficult to value and can be difficult to sell.

In assessing the required margin, the dominant factor will be how possible it is to establish the realisation value of the security. On the face of it, quoted shares are easy to value but the quoted price assumes a ready buyer at that level. This may hold true for small amounts of shares but cannot be assumed for large blocks, especially in smaller companies.

The sale of a large block of shares in a company could of itself depress the share price. If this is the case, the price quoted by stock brokers will not be obtained on a sale and a wide margin—usually around 100%—will be needed.

If the sale will not affect the share price, then the margin calculation will be governed by a more general assessment of the volatility of the value of the sales over the term of the lending. The general state of the stock market will have to be taken into account. The October 1987 'Crash' showed how quickly share prices could fall in a short period when the market generally had reached a peak. Lenders will have to decide whether the basic proposition warrants having sufficient security cover to meet this kind of 'catastrophe'. However, assuming a generally stable stock market—a big 'if'—and assuming monitoring of the security, say, every two weeks, the following margins should be sufficient to cover general price falls:

Security	Recommended minimum margin
UK gilts—short & long date	5%
UK equities	15%
Bonds (corporate, local authority and bulldog)	5%
Debentures/loan stocks	10%
Covertible loan stocks/preference shares	15%

Note—USM stocks will require a wider margin.

The possibility of depreciation is greater over a longer period and a larger margin would be required if less regular monitoring is to take place. Higher margins may also be appropriate for particular shares and reference to the 'Highs' and 'Lows' column of the Financial Times will give a useful guide to past volatility in price, although it has to be said that this can be no guarantee of future movements.

Finally, it will be prudent to add a further 5% to whatever security margin is deemed necessary to cover price falls and to cater for potential rolled up interest.

(C) PROPERTY VALUATIONS

Lenders are not expert property valuers and cannot view a property with the skill of the professional valuer. Some properties are difficult to value because of their specialised nature or location, and others might require a detailed internal inspection.

Lenders are sometimes tempted to put a 'ball park' valuation on a property, particularly when the borrower resists paying the cost of a professional valuation. Such an approach may be satisfactory when lending only a small amount but when the security is being relied on for a significant sum, the services of a professional valuer are essential.

Renewal of Valuations

Under normal circumstances it is prudent to re-value security every three years, although there will be occasions when it should be done more frequently. This would usually be required when the lender's risk was high.

By the same token, if a lending is being repaid satisfactorily or if security is relied on for only a small proportion of its value, revaluation can be dispensed with unless the area in which the property is located is showing a serious decline in property values generally.

(D)   SECOND MORTGAGES

Second mortgages over houses are one of the most common forms of security taken by lending institutions. There is a tendency to regard all second charges as being of a similar quality but this is incorrect as some represent better security than others.

Value of the Equity

Of crucial importance when assessing the value of a second charge is the relationship between the amount of the prior charges and the size of the equity available to the lender.

In order to realise the security, a lender would have to pay off prior mortgages. The more usual alternative is that the lender sits tight and waits for the first mortgagee to sell the property—presumably their loan is not being repaid either. The disadvantage of this alternative is that whilst the first mortgagee is obliged to get the best price possible for the property, his prime concern will be to obtain repayment of his own debt, not that of subsequent mortgagees.

Earlier in this chapter, the size of the security margin necessary on property was discussed. In order for a second or subsequent mortgage to fully secure a borrowing, a larger margin will be needed than where a first charge is concerned. It has to be remembered that it would be the second mortgagee's equity which would bear the brunt of any reduction in the value of the property and/or the roll up of interest (on all mortgages—not just the lender's own). Where the total of prior mortgages exceeds the recommended 80% set out in the Security Margins section above, the lender should regard the second charge as being of minimal value only.

However, the lender's position is much stronger where prior mortgages are small in relation to the overall property value. A lender may be willing to repay a small first mortgage in order to control a forced sale and an acceptable security margin is much more likely to be achieved.

Matrimonial Homes

Special problems can be posed when matrimonial homes are taken as security, especially where the borrowing to be secured is not directly related to the purchase or improvement of the property. This is because the mortgagor may be reluctant to sacrifice the family home to see a lender repaid following failure of his or her business.

It is not prudent to lend against a second or subsequent mortgage on a matrimonial home to an extent where the mortgagor would lose everything if the lender realised the security. A larger margin than the 20% mentioned above in relation to residential property should be considered so that, if things go wrong, the mortgagor will still have some cash left over to put down as a deposit on a new property, following the sale of the old. It is good policy to leave the borrower some room to start again as this will make the realisation of security a much less painful business all round.

(E) GUARANTEES AND OTHER THIRD PARTY SECURITY

This section will deal with some of the practical aspects of taking guarantees.

It is vital that a guarantor fully understands the nature and extent of the liability being undertaken. The courts have accepted that banks can themselves explain the effect of the security to a potential guarantor, but the explanation must not mislead the guarantor. For example, when a third party mortgage taken to secure an overdraft was described as 'like a building society mortgage' the court held that the description was negligent, and the bank concerned was held liable to pay damages.

The following points are particularly important:

(a) The 'all monies' clause in bank charge forms can only be relied upon if the guarantor has been made fully aware of it, and accepts unlimited liability. Unless this is done, it is highly likely that the bank will be challenged if reliance is placed on third party security for any increase in lending or new facilities where it was originally taken to secure a specific arrangement. In the absence of evidence of agreement to unlimited liability, it would be prudent to obtain the guarantor's written agreement before advancing further monies.

(b) Where the guarantor obtains no benefit from entering into the liability, it is of special importance that the nature and extent of the liability is fully understood. The opportunity to seek independent legal advice should be extended, where required.

(c) The guarantor should be advised to consult a solicitor if there is any suspicion that he or she has been influenced by the borrower or by anyone else, or if any doubt remains concerning his or her appreciation of the guarantee's implications.

(d) Independent legal advice will be necessary where there is a special relationship between debtor and guarantor, which enables the debtor to influence the guarantor's actions, for example parent/ child, doctor/patient, etc. Whilst husband and wife are not included in this category, care must be exercised in all cases where guarantees or other third party security are taken where this relationship exists. This is especially important when the guarantor is not in a position to control the principal debtor's borrowing.

(e) Lending institutions with a branch network must ensure that, where a guarantee or charge form is to be signed at a different branch from the one where the lending takes place, the other branch is given sufficient information to allow an adequate explanation to be given of the liability being undertaken.

(f) Advice should be restricted to explaining the effect of the charge and the nature and extent of the liability. If advice is sought on the wisdom of undertaking a liability, the guarantor should be advised to consult a solicitor.

(g) Where a director is giving an unsupported guarantee for a company's liabilities, the possible consequences of the wrongful trading provisions of the Insolvency Act should be considered. It is possible that a director could incur full liability for the company's debts in a wrongful trading situation. The value of large unsupported guarantees is often doubtful because it is taken on trust that personal assets are owned by the individual concerned, and switching can take place without the lender being aware. Where heavy reliance is placed on a large guarantee, it should be supported by tangible security.

5 PERSONAL BORROWERS — WHEN THINGS GO WRONG

This chapter examines the sort of action a lender might take in dealing with personal borrowers who get into difficulties.

The following aspects will be considered:

(a) Identifying problem accounts
(b) Dealing with problem accounts
(c) Rescheduling a debt
(d) Recovery procedures
(e) Legal proceedings.

(A) IDENTIFYING PROBLEM ACCOUNTS

Information which leads a lender to suspect that a borrower is in financial difficulty can come from many sources but will usually arise from carrying out the monitoring and control procedures suggested in Chapter 2. When a problem becomes apparent the lender needs to take immediate action as letting matters drift will be in nobody's interest. Some of the situations which may indicate financial problems on the part of a customer are as follows:

(a) an overdraft being taken above the agreed limit;
(b) an overdraft being taken in excess of an unadvised limit—the customer will not know that such a limit exists and the whole balance needs to be reviewed;
(c) an account goes overdrawn where no limit is marked;
(d) cheques paid into an account are returned unpaid leaving an overdraft—this may be an indication of cross-firing (see Chapter 9);
(e) an agreed overdraft is not repaid on time;
(f) a loan repayment is not received on time or some other agreed condition of the facility is not met;
(g) an overdraft is taken on an account which has not operated for some time;

(h) no credit has been received for an account for, say, six weeks— has the customer's salary stopped?

(i) the balance of an overdraft where an unadvised limit is marked shows a rising trend over a period of months.

There may be a satisfactory explanation for any one of the above situations occurring, but they are an indication of something which has gone wrong and an investigation of an account going overdrawn above a limit may identify another warning sign such as an increasing trend in the balance. The particular warning sign may be simply the tip of the iceberg.

Clearly the lender needs to be amount conscious when deciding whether to carry out a detailed review of an account, but if a review is not to be undertaken when a warning sign appears, it should be based on a definite decision, not just 'masterly inaction'.

(B) DEALING WITH PROBLEM ACCOUNTS

The first step to be taken when a problem becomes apparent will generally be to contact the customer by letter or telephone. If no response is received, firmer action will be necessary which needs to both follow a strict timetable and adopt a logical approach.

The initial letter should request either funds to correct the position or contact from a customer so that the problem can be discussed. A reasonable period needs to be given for the customer to respond, say two weeks. Further action will then be necessary. This will probably take the form of a stronger letter or an attempt at telephone contact. The refusal of the customer to respond to the first letter is a further warning sign and the lender should now consider tougher action such as:

(a) returning cheques (this does not of course mean that the lender is in any way precluded from returning cheques at an earlier stage if it is felt necessary);

(b) cancelling standing order and direct debit mandates;

(c) cancelling any unadvised limit;

(d) requesting the return of the customer's cheque book;

(e) requesting the return of the customer's cheque guarantee card, etc;

(f) cancelling open credits;

(g) searching with a Credit Reference Agency.

The lender must avoid sending a steadily increasing number of threatening letters but then doing nothing. The persistent debtor will quickly become used to receiving them and it will be logical for him or her to simply ignore them.

Telephone Contact

Where letters are being ignored or more urgent contact with the customer is needed, contact by telephone will probably be the best course. General experience suggests that telephoning produces a better response than sending letters. The reason for this is obvious; on the telephone there is the ability to have two way contact which can lead to a greater understanding of the customer's problem and a commitment to do something about it.

The telephone call should not be made in a haphazard manner. The objectives of the call must be clear before it is made. The objectives will usually be:

(a) to establish contact and to check the customer's address in case a previous letter has not been received and provide the basis for future action;

(b) to obtain a commitment to correct the overdraft or rectify the position on a loan account, etc., or to establish a realistic repayment programme;

(c) if adjustment is not possible, to establish why this is so;

(d) to inform a customer of the consequences should he or she fail to meet the lender's request. Great care should be taken to avoid accusations of harassment;

(e) to obtain an up to date picture of the customer's general financial circumstances including details of employment, assets, liabilities, income and expenditure.

To achieve the above objectives good preparation is essential. A meaningful dialogue will not be possible if the facts of a customer's situation become a matter of dispute. The lender must be in a position to answer any questions relating to the recent history of the account.

A positive and confident attitude must be adopted. It is a great mistake for the lender to lose his or her temper with a customer, even if provoked, as this will lose the initiative to the debtor. A firm but polite tone must be adopted and above all, the lender must not be diverted from the objectives of the call.

It will usually be possible to get some sort of commitment from the customer, if only to a small payment. An immediate note should be made of any agreement and this should be followed up by a letter to the customer confirming the details so that there can be no dispute in the future.

Finally, the customer's promise to repay must be monitored to ensure that the agreement is honoured.

(C) RESCHEDULING A DEBT

The discussions with a customer may show that he or she will not be able to repay the borrowing as originally envisaged. The customer may request a longer period to pay and may also suggest that the lender takes on other debts where creditors are pressing. In such circumstances any future lending will involve a high degree of risk and greater caution will be required.

The following approach should be adopted:

(a) Obtain a full list of the customer's present commitments and income.
(b) If a significant over-commitment is identified, the possibility of reducing it needs to be considered, for example, by re-negotiating with other lenders or sale of assets.
(c) A review of the customer's assets should be undertaken to establish if there are any which may be sold to reduce the debt or alternatively offered as security in return for consolidating overall commitments or extending the repayment terms.
(d) Where it is apparent that the customer is genuinely over-committed and asset sales are not possible to reduce the borrowing, consideration might be given to reducing the overall monthly repayments by amalgamating other debts with the lender's own borrowing with a repayment programme that the customer should be able to afford. The term of such an arrangement will almost certainly be less than ideal and the risk in the lending will be significant, so that if the borrowing is of any size, the lender should insist upon taking security.
(e) The customer must understand that rescheduling is a course of last resort and that if any further problems arise an immediate discussion with the lender will be necessary.
(f) The lending should be by way of loan account which should be subject to regular review so that repayments may be increased in the future. A higher interest rate than previously ought to be charged to reflect the higher risk although it might be suggested that this could be reduced if the repayment rate is increased in the future.
(g) No further overdrafts should be allowed and it should be a condition that no borrowing should be taken elsewhere without the lender's agreement. It may be necessary therefore to insist that the customer's credit cards, etc., are cancelled and the cheque guarantee facility withdrawn.

(D)   RECOVERY PROCEDURES

When despite every attempt by the lender to reach an amicable arrangement for repayment of a borrowing, no agreement has been possible, it will be necessary to treat the borrowing as a recovery matter. Eventually, resort may have to be made to legal proceedings against the borrower. Lenders generally will wish to avoid this if at all possible.

It is easy for a lender to become emotional about the recovery of doubtful debts as the lender may feel personally 'let down'. It is important to keep the following considerations in mind:

(a)   The lender must seek to control the situation and adopt a positive approach at all times.

(b)   There must be a clearly defined objective. Ideally this will be the full repayment of the borrowing but, where the borrower's circumstances make this impossible, the aim should be to achieve the maximum possible recovery.

(c)   There must be a logical approach to the problem.

(d)   Actions must be carried through. There is no point bluffing and if a threat is made it must be followed up.

(e)   Whilst endeavouring to make the maximum recovery, the lender must not lose a sense of proportion and if there are mitigating circumstances, for example, if the borrower is handicapped, a sense of social responsibility needs to be shown.

(f)   A clear idea of the costs of recovery must be borne in mind. There is no point in pursuing the debt if the cost of doing so will exceed or approach the amount involved.

Before commencing legal proceedings there are a number of steps which the lender should take:

(a)   Check any security to see that it has been properly charged and can be sold if necessary.

(b)   Make one last attempt to correspond with the debtor to try to reach a reasonable agreement for the repayment of the debts.

(c)   Make a last attempt to arrange a meeting perhaps at the borrower's home so that a view can be obtained of his or her financial status which may help in the decision on what course of legal proceedings to take. Care needs to be exercised when visiting customers that no accusation of duress can be raised and it is strongly recommended therefore that visits are always undertaken by two representatives of the lender.

(d)   Formal demand should be made. The court will look to see if this has been done and due regard must be taken of the requirements of the Consumer Credit Act if the borrowing is 'regulated' as defined in the Act.

(e) It may be necessary to use the services of either investigators or tracing agents. An investigator would be used to find out what assets and liabilities the borrower has which might be sold to repay the lender. Tracing agents would be employed to find a customer with whom the lender has lost contact.

(f) Whilst full recovery will be the aim, it may be sensible to agree a settlement with the borrower to avoid the cost of legal proceedings. This will involve the lender in writing off part of the debt but the outcome of legal proceedings may not be certain and 'a bird in the hand is worth two in the bush'.

(E) LEGAL PROCEEDINGS

If satisfactory arrangements for repayment cannot be arranged with the borrower, then the lender will have to start legal proceedings. However, the lender must always be ready to re-open negotiations with the debtor if it is thought that a better chance of recovery exists by doing so. In such circumstances, care needs to be taken that the debtor is not merely using delaying tactics.

The kinds of legal proceedings which can be taken are as follows:

Solicitor's Letter

The lender instructs a solicitor to write to the debtor stating that the lender would still like to reach a satisfactory agreement in respect of repayment of the debt, but if this is not forthcoming then legal proceedings will commence. The debtor is usually given around 14 days in which to respond but if no response is received, the lender must proceed to the next step.

Sworn Statement of Affairs

If a debtor is agreeable, he or she may be prepared to give a statement of assets, liabilities, income and expenditure under oath in the presence of a solicitor or Commissioner for Oaths. This will only be of value if the debtor can be trusted. It would form an essential part of any settlement with the debtor for a sum less than the full amount of the liability.

Mareva Injunction

This is a court order which freezes the debtor's assets, i.e. prevents him or her selling them or taking them out of the lender's reach.

The lender will not be able to obtain any particular hold over the assets and will need to follow up the injunction with judgment and some other form of action to gain control of them.

Great care needs to be taken before obtaining a Mareva injunction, since if it is subsequently held that the lender acted irresponsibly, then a claim for damages might result.

Judgment

This is the legal recognition of the lender's debt and must be obtained before the lender can exercise its legal remedies against the debtor. If the lender holds security, it can still be realised either before or after judgment has been obtained.

Judgment can be obtained in either the County Court or the High Court and will usually be preceded by a solicitor issuing a Default Summons (i.e. formal notification that the debtor has defaulted in meeting formal demand for repayment of the debt). The County Court is normally used for debts up to £5,000 as proceedings in the High Courts are more expensive but there may be circumstances where it may be considered appropriate to proceed in the High Court for smaller sums.

Instalment Orders

The debtor can apply to the court for an order to repay the judgment debt by instalments. The lender will have to accept this method no matter how small are the instalments set by the court.

Oral Examination

This is an examination in the court after judgment has been obtained to discover the debtor's assets and liabilities, income and expenditure. It can reveal assets which the lender did not know about. Furthermore the embarrassment of a court hearing might persuade the debtor to offer repayment proposals acceptable to the lender before legal action is taken.

Enforcing the Judgment

Once judgment has been obtained the lender has to decide which remedy for the recovery of the debt will be most appropriate. This will depend on the size of the debt and the debtor's assets and liabilities. The remedies most commonly available are:

(a) *Attachment of earnings order.* This is an order available only through the County Court (not the High Court) which instructs the debtor's employers to deduct a fixed sum from the debtor's wages/salary and to pay the money into court and eventually to the lender.

The court decides the level of pay which the debtor needs for normal living expenses—these are called 'protected earnings'. Only amounts in excess of this figure will be subject to the order.

The system is unpopular with employers because of the amount of administration involved and can be defeated by the debtor becoming self-employed, changing jobs or being made redundant.

(b) *Charging orders.* A lender can apply for a charging order over any land or stocks and shares owned by the debtor. This will be useful in those situations where the lender does not hold any assets as security but knows they exist. The charging order gives the lender the same powers as an equitable charge, i.e. no power of sale but if the asset is sold, the lender will receive the proceeds.

(c) *Receiver by way of equitable execution.* This remedy applies to assets not covered by charging orders, the main one of which will be life policies. The effect of the order is that when the asset is sold the debtor's share of the proceeds is available to the lender. The lender has no power to insist on the surrender of a life policy and, to be safe, will need to obtain a court injunction to prevent the debtor from dealing with the asset.

(d) *Garnishee orders.* This is an order served on a third party who owes money to the debtor and it prevents the third party from making payment to the debtor. Instead payment has to be made to the court for the benefit of the lender. For example if the lender discovers that the debtor has a credit balance with another bank or building society, a garnishee order can be issued on the other bank thus freezing the credit balance.

The application for a garnishee order is in two stages. First, an order nisi is served on the third party and then on the debtor—this is so as not to warn the debtor and give him or her the opportunity to withdraw the balance. If there is no objection the order is then made absolute.

(e) *Levying execution.* This remedy is used when the lender wants to obtain and sell the debtor's goods, for example a car or other household goods.

The lender obtains a warrant of execution (County Court) or a writ of *Fieri Facias* (High Court) which involves a bailiff or sheriff seizing the debtor's goods and selling them to meet the debt.

The threat of a bailiff or sheriff calling can sometimes persuade the debtor to contact the bank with proposals for repayment.

(f) *Bankruptcy.* This is a serious step for a lender to take as it puts severe restrictions on a debtor's personal and business life.

From a lender's point of view, bankruptcy is not always the most logical way to proceed as a debtor's assets become available to all creditors and not just the lender. For this reason, if possible, other steps should be taken to attach any available assets prior to considering bankruptcy.

(g) *Voluntary arrangements.* Under the Insolvency Act 1986 a debtor can put forward proposals for partial settlement of his or her debts—this is known as a voluntary arrangement.

Such an arrangement must be agreed by three quarters (by value) of the debtor's creditors.

PART C

CORPORATE LENDING

6 SMALL CORPORATE LENDING

The common ways in which distinctions are drawn between large and small businesses are number of employees, size of sales turnover, size of capital base, etc. For the lender these distinctions are not as important as the fact that many 'small' businesses either cannot or will not produce good quality management information or projections which are generally available from 'larger' ones. The lender needs to adopt a different approach to these two categories of business.

Some people believe that the managers of 'small businesses' should be educated into producing the sort of information which the lender wants. Experience suggests that this is not always possible. This chapter will concentrate on those businesses which are either unable or unwilling to provide good quality financial information. The subject matter will be examined under the following headings:

(a) Limitations of some customer-generated information
(b) Appraising business proposals without good quality financial information
(c) Uncertainty and security
(d) Monitoring and control
(e) Small firms loan guarantee scheme.

(A) LIMITATIONS OF SOME CUSTOMER-GENERATED INFORMATION

Ideally, small businesses would have efficient systems for collecting together information and for forecasting so that they would be able to keep themselves and the lender up to date with their present financial position and prospects. Unfortunately, in practice, such arrangements tend to be the exception rather than the rule. Although it might be possible to convince some of them of the benefits of formal management information systems, in the majority of cases the lender will usually have to make do with the information that they will or can provide.

When pressed to do so, small businesses will produce formal budgets and cash flow forecasts. Where they cannot do this for themselves they will have no difficulty in enlisting the help of an outside accountant. The accountant will be working for the customer, not the bank, and will therefore wish to keep the customer, rather than the bank, happy. Such forecasts will tend to show that the facility being requested is needed and that it can be repaid.

It is not unreasonable for the lender to treat with suspicion cash flow forecasts and budgets which have been prepared by, or at the request of, businesses which would not usually undertake any formal financial planning. Sales forecasts in such projections are often over-optimistic and the lender cannot expect outside accountants to curb the optimism of their clients (although that is not to say some good ones will not try).

Cash flow forecasts which are drawn up to 'prove a point' are easily prepared from the bottom line upwards so that the sales receipts line at the top shows what is necessary to produce the required result in terms of cash flow at the bottom. This may be a useful technique for calculating target sales, but is dangerous if no thought is given to whether such sales levels are actually achievable. Such forecasts are of little use to a lender who must always focus on what the real future out turn is likely to be.

A lender who insists on detailed projections from unsophisticated businesses can be faced with awkward consequences. It can be difficult to decline a proposition which a lender instinctively recognises as being unsound when faced with a budget and/or cashflow forecast which mathematically indicates otherwise.

This instinctive unease with the proposition will usually be caused by the difficulty in testing the assumptions on which the figures are based. In particular, the sales assumptions will be critical but, more often than not, the lender will have little more than a customer's word that they are achievable. It is simply not possible with small businesses, to seek independent verification by way of market surveys, etc.

Given that the motive behind documents produced by accountants is usually to maximise the chances of their clients obtaining the loan, the lender must concentrate on distinguishing between the story told in often impressive looking documents and the underlying soundness of the proposition.

Scepticism will always be in order when forecasts are produced which are significantly different from recent actual results. Good common sense reasons need to be put forward to justify any improvement. The one piece of factual evidence which the lender will have is the borrower's track record and this will always be an important ingredient in the appraisal.

The problems caused by the high degree of uncertainty surrounding small business propositions will tend to lead a lender to look for security. The provision of security will often play a major role in making small business propositions acceptable, but the fact that it is available should not blind the lender to the need to form a judgment on underlying viability. Assessment does not necessarily have to be detailed or sophisticated. Provided the key variables are considered, a very rough calculation may suffice for the initial appraisal and will provide a basis for subsequent monitoring.

(B) APPRAISING BUSINESS PROPOSALS WITHOUT GOOD QUALITY FINANCIAL INFORMATION

Borrowers with both the integrity and capacity to draw a detailed, reliable business plan and to follow it up with the provision of good quality monitoring information can be approached on the basis outlined in Chapter 7. However, if the borrower lacks integrity, expertise or resources, the reliance on such an approach may be dangerous for the lender.

Taking decisions as to whether to lend to small businesses against the background of inadequate information is a task which even the most experienced of lenders finds demanding. In those situations where serious doubts exist about the viability of a proposition, it will usually be wise to seek a second opinion from a colleague whose judgment and objectivity is respected.

The canons of good lending and the approach set out in Chapter 1 will form the basis of appraisal. However the particular difficulty in connection with small business appraisal is the scarcity of independent evidence to support the key assumptions which will form the basis of the proposition.

What evidence should be available in such situations? The areas which need to be examined are:

(a) the ability and integrity of the proprietors;
(b) the availability of physical and production resources;
(c) the present and potential profitability;
(d) the impact of the proposition on future cashflow;
(e) the adequacy of present and planned capital resources.

Ability and Integrity of Proprietors

The lender must aim to form an opinion of the ability of the proprietors and management to run a successful business and to make reasonable forecasts of its future. It is a dangerous delusion to believe somebody's integrity and management ability can be assessed on the basis of a short meeting. Facts are needed and these will be provided by the proprietor's past performance. Particular attention should be paid to the following areas:

(a) How long has the borrower been known? What is the borrower's track record?
(b) If not known to the lender before, why is the borrower making the approach? Can evidence be shown of an acceptable track record elsewhere?
(c) Has the borrower complied with previous borrowing arrangements (both business and personal). Bank statements ought to be provided by non-customers.
(d) What is the borrower worth financially?
(e) How has personal worth been accumulated—own efforts, inheritance or simply inflation in property prices?
(f) Does the borrower have any experience of running a business?
(g) Is the borrower experienced in the particular trade which is the subject of the advance?
(h) If the customer is new, a curriculum vitae should be supplied.
(i) How great is the borrower's personal commitment to the business? Is a personal guarantee being offered where the borrower is a limited company?
(j) Does the borrower have adequate life and health cover?

Availability of Physical and Production Resources

It should not automatically be assumed that the borrower has adequate premises and plant to carry out the planned objectives. A visit to the borrower's premises is usually essential as the only way to get first hand evidence. This means that where the bank or lending organisation has a branch network, it is going to be more cost effective for a distant borrower to be dealt with through a local branch. The banks' bad debt records in relation to 'distant borrowers' are worse than for those which bank locally. The temptation to take on business no matter where it is located needs to be resisted.

The composition of the borrower's physical resources can be a useful indicator of his or her business philosophy. Excessively luxurious premises or—and this can be very common—an ostentatious motor car, may suggest an irresponsible approach to the use of scarce capital resources and should serve as a warning sign.

Conversely, too frugal an attitude to essential plant and equipment could create future problems with machines breaking down, which will in turn affect production and costs. A common sense approach to the following key areas is required.

(a) Are the premises the right size and in the best location?

(b) What are the key elements of plant and machinery?
(c) Are spare parts available for ageing equipment—what is the cost of replacement, and does the borrower have sufficient expertise on the payroll to make mechanical repairs?
(d) Is existing plant adequate to satisfy planned production, and what would be the cost of expansion beyond present capacity?
(e) Is there a sufficient supply of labour of the right quality?
(f) Are key personnel well paid and how difficult would it be to replace them?

Present and Potential Profitability

Historical accounts should be available to be analysed for all businesses except new ventures. The standard of accounts can vary widely. Lenders are often told that they have been prepared for 'tax purposes' and that the true performance of the business is, in reality, much better. There is an argument for treating such accounts as being an accurate representation of the business's performance, but the practice of producing accounts 'for the tax man' is so widespread that this approach is not helpful. The important thing which a lender wishes to establish is the true financial position of the business and its real cash generating capacity.

The most widely practised ways of reducing profit for tax purposes are understating the value of closing stock and taking cash 'out of the till' so that part of the sales income does not pass through the business's books. Unless it is practical to have an independent valuation of stock carried out, there is no easy way to assess whether stock is actually undervalued. However, if cash is being taken out of a business without appearing in the books, it is not unreasonable to seek evidence as to where it has gone. Such cash must represent surplus income over and above the amount the proprietor needs to maintain a reasonable life style. In a small business a reasonable level of income for the proprietor is one of the costs which must always be borne if the company is to have a stable future. Cash taken out of a business which forms part of the proprietor's normal income cannot be regarded as a hidden profit available to repay borrowing, unless it has been either saved in some way or spent on 'luxuries'. Evidence of such saving or expenditure may be available.

A lender would not expect to see a business which is supposedly generating more cash and profit than is passing through the books to be working close to its overdraft limit and an examination of past bank statements showing the run of the bank account can be an informative exercise.

In addition to examining the historic audited accounts, it will be necessary to look at the more recent trading performance of the business. By definition there will be no management accounts and it is by no means unusual to find the last set of audited accounts to be very historic. The lender can, however, in the case of most businesses, ask to see the quarterly VAT returns which will provide evidence of recent sales. VAT returns have to be sent to Customs and Excise within one month of the quarter ending, and failure to do so could involve the business in heavy penalties. A lender should be suspicious if a business accounts for VAT quarterly, but copies of returns are not available. (It should be noted that some businesses account for VAT monthly, but in such instances a level of sales is assumed so that the returns will not be good evidence of actual achievement.)

In the absence of formal budgets and cash flow forecasts, the lender will need to do some basic sums to assess the effects of the borrower's plans. A simple break-even analysis, estimating profitability in relation to a range of possible future sales levels, can be a useful tool. The borrower ought to be able to provide approximate figures for future overheads and other fixed costs together with an assessment of the sort of gross margin expected to be achieved on sales. A good small trader will always have a good idea of basic business costs and prices even though these will not normally be formally recorded. If the borrower is unable to provide even this rudimentary information, and to justify it in the face of testing questioning, then the lender should be very cautious.

Once sufficient information has been provided to establish the level of sales needed to generate an acceptable level of profit, the lender will have to judge, on the basis of the business's past performance and the lender's own knowledge of the market, whether the target and, therefore the whole proposition, is viable.

Liquidity and Cash Needs

With existing customers the evidence of past liquidity can be seen from the pattern of their bank account. Non-customers should always be asked to provide their bank statements. The lender needs to know how comfortably past borrowing has been kept within arrangements. Suggestions of past pressure on limits should be a cause for caution and downright suspicion if there is evidence of cheques being returned, no matter what excuses are given.

Generally speaking, small businesses are not in a position to dictate credit terms to either their customers or suppliers. It is important therefore that suppliers are paid promptly if a reasonable period of credit taken is to be maintained. Again the treatment of VAT returns can give a useful insight into whether payment of creditors is being delayed. VAT has to be paid within one month following the submission of the quarterly return and heavy surcharges can be imposed on businesses which regularly pay late. The severity of these surcharges means that businesses are unlikely, voluntarily, to delay payment of VAT and slow payment will be a warning sign.

The borrower who tries to predict future requirements without the aid of a formal cash flow forecast will merely have made a 'best estimate'. This must be tested and the borrower should be questioned about the assumptions made. It may be possible for the borrower's estimate to be quite close. Most businesses have a pattern of repetitive payments within a short timescale, e.g. wages, superimposed on another pattern of less regular payments to creditors and receipts from sales.

The borrower needs to have a fundamental understanding of these patterns and the relationship between credit given and taken if an accurate estimate of cash needs is to be made. The lender's questions need to focus on these areas and caution needs to be exercised if satisfactory answers are not given.

Further questions need to be asked to test the degree of flexibility the borrower has to run the business within the confines of a particular overdraft limit. If things do not go according to plan, can the borrower change the level of operations and/or the timing of payments to creditors to ensure the limit will not be exceeded? If the borrower does not have much flexibility, the lender must be prepared to agree a limit to meet a worst case situation if the proposition is to be acceptable.

Adequacy of Capital Resources

Lenders will want to see a reasonable level of capital in a business both as evidence of the borrower's commitment and as a buffer against loss. If a borrower is able to contribute a significant capital stake, it may indicate evidence of past achievements which will give the lender confidence that future plans also can be brought to fruition.

Some lenders are prepared to argue that a director's guarantee supported by a charge over personal assets can be regarded as a substitute for capital. Whilst such a guarantee is evidence of commitment, it is a poor substitute for a reasonable level of capital resources. This is because inadequate proprietor's capital will result in a business having a significant borrowing requirement, the interest cost of which will raise the business's break-even point. Moreover, if profits are not earned, proprietor's capital does not have to be repaid whereas both interest and borrowing do.

A business with a low capital base will have to generate a significantly higher level of sales in order to survive than one which is adequately capitalised. The lender will therefore need to be particularly wary of propositions from poorly capitalised businesses, even though apparently good third party security might be offered.

(C)   UNCERTAINTY AND SECURITY

Even when the lender has carried out all the tests and asked the sort of questions suggested above, it is still likely that significant doubts will remain concerning the viability of the plans of many unsophisticated small businesses. The assessment of the probability of a business meeting sales targets will be based on the lender's own subjective judgment of the market rather than hard evidence.

Whilst on balance a lender may feel that a plan is attainable, confidence in that judgment may not be great and there will remain a significant possibility of things going wrong. Fundamentally, it will be difficult to be sure that repayment will be achieved. Small businesses are often vulnerable to events outside their control, many of which can be difficult to foresee. It will be more by good luck than good judgment that a lender will cover such factors in the evaluation of the proposition. To give an example, the Chernobyl nuclear accident caused severe difficulties for Welsh sheep farmers; it is highly unlikely that Welsh bank managers had brought the implications of this particular event into their calculations. What could have been foreseen in advance is that some farmers would be more vulnerable than others. The vulnerability of small firms to unforeseen events is a result of their limited capital resources being insufficient to withstand what might be only a temporary problem. If a small business is not well capitalised, it is likely that cover against potential loss will require the lender to be fully secured with a good margin.

Although there will be exceptions, it is usually prudent to take personal guarantees from directors when lending to small companies. It is difficult to separate the small company from its proprietors and experience has shown that, when a guarantee has been given, the directors do demonstrate a more responsible attitude to the risk they are prepared to take with borrowed money. The high failure rate apparent under the government's Small Firms Loan Guarantee Scheme indicates what can happen when directors are not tied in by guarantees.

A request for a guarantee can also be justified on the basis that, whilst the potential rewards in the business go to the proprietor, the potential losses will fall on the lender.

Some guarantees may be taken for moral purposes only but, where reliance is to be placed on them as security, they should be supported by tangible assets. The only exceptions to this rule should be where the lender is absolutely satisfied that the individual concerned will prove good for the guarantee liability on an unsupported basis. The apparent existence of wealth should not be sufficient in itself as many apparently rich people have their assets tied up in trusts, etc. The lender should not be coy about seeking evidence of the exact ownership of wealth when taking this sort of decision.

Chapters 4 and 8 deal with what constitutes a good security margin. If it is not possible to obtain an adequate margin, the lender should realise that the decision is based on the acceptance of a partly unsecured position.

Assets taken as security and any other key elements of the business should be adequately insured (including loss of profits). Businesses with limited capital resources are not in a position to cope with unexpected disasters, so those events which can be insured against should be covered.

(D) MONITORING AND CONTROL

This aspect is dealt with in more detail in Chapter 7 under the same sub-heading. The following comments should be read in conjunction with that section.

The lender should not expect information provided by the borrower for monitoring purposes to be more than basic. The lending facilities should therefore be structured in a way which will assist a lender in controlling the advance and, at the same time, help the borrower maintain financial discipline. As far as possible, lending should be by way of loan rather than overdraft. This not only establishes an automatic mechanism for monitoring repayment, but also enables the lender to ensure that the facility is used only for the purpose for which it was granted.

The borrower should be asked to supply copies of quarterly VAT returns where appropriate, so that the level of sales can be monitored along with proof of prompt payment of VAT. All businesses ought to be able to provide monthly sales figures without difficulty and, if advance orders make up an important element of sales, copies of these should also be provided on a regular basis.

With some businesses there will be important non-financial indicators of performance which can also be monitored. To give some examples: the level of bed occupancy for a hotel or nursing home; numbers of customers served for a restaurant; number of staff out on jobs for a temporary employment agency. The proprietors of such businesses ought to know these key figures and be able to give a reasoned estimate of the break-even level of operations to give a basis for future monitoring.

Lenders need to avoid the trap of hoping for the best where small customers are concerned. If unexpected adverse trends are seen in monitoring information, it is vital that the customer is questioned and any necessary action is taken. The need to be objective when problems are apparent is paramount; the borrower and the lender are both likely to be worse off if early remedial action is not taken.

(E)   SMALL FIRMS LOAN GUARANTEE SCHEME

This scheme was established in 1981 to make finance available to businesses where a lender would not normally be willing to grant a facility under one of its own loan schemes without the benefit of a government guarantee.

Funds can be used for capital expenditure, working capital or project development costs. All manufacturing businesses are eligible as well as many service businesses (there is a list of ineligible businesses) and loans can be granted for sums between £5,000 minimum to £75,000 maximum. The term can be between two and seven years with repayment being by equal monthly or quarterly instalments, although a capital repayment holiday of up to two years may be agreed.

The security for loans is a guarantee by the Secretary of State for Industry for 70% of the reducing loan balance. Where assets employed in the business are capable of being charged on standard bank forms, the provision of such security will be a conditon of the loan. Thus in the case of a company, a debenture will be expected. The guaranteed and non guaranteed portions of the loan will rank pro rata, pari passu against the debenture security.

By definition loans granted under the scheme involve a greater degree of risk than a lender is usually prepared to accept. Evaluation is therefore difficult and is complicated by the paradox of first having to decline the proposition on normal banking grounds, before then deciding it is sufficiently viable to be agreed under the scheme.

To qualify for the scheme, businesses must appear to be soundly based and have a fair chance of success, whilst also being unable to raise finance because of high gearing and/or the lack of adequate security. The provision of security provided by the government guarantee does not obviate the need for a detailed analysis of the proposition, indeed the high level of risk means that the appraisal should be more rigorous than usual. Applicants under the scheme more often than not fall into the category of individuals covered by this chapter, and the appraisal procedures in earlier sections need to be followed.

The taking of a personal guarantee to cover the scheme borrowing is prohibited. This means that it is possible for a participant to walk away from a business if things go wrong at an early stage with only a limited personal loss. The lender needs to give particular attention to the assessment of the participant's commitment to the business and, if there are any doubts, should not proceed with the facility.

The scheme allows for high gearing as well as the absence of security. The high level of finance charges associated with high gearing—and interest rates typically charged by lenders operating the scheme are not cheap—will make it very difficult for the business to service its debt and survive if its projections prove wrong. The Robson Rhodes analysis of scheme failures published in 1983 indicated that start-ups would have to have unusually good prospects if they were to be geared up more than 5:1. The continued high failure rate since 1983 suggests that this figure could be over generous.

7 LARGE CORPORATE LENDING

In this chapter, an examination will be made of those businesses which can provide detailed information to enable a lender to make an assessment of the borrower and the proposition.

It will be assumed that the reader is familiar with accounting ratios and the principles of management accounting. If not, then reference should be made to the following books:

Accountancy for Banking Students—Edwards and Mellett
Interpretation of Balance Sheets—Hutchinson and Dyer
Balance Sheets and the Lending Banker—Clemens and Dyer
Management Accounting for the Lending Banker—Pitcher

The content of this chapter will be dealt with under the following headings:

(a) Appraising a business
(b) Capital investment appraisal
(c) Appraising profit forecasts
(d) Appraising liquidity forecasts
(e) Monitoring and control
(f) Medium term lending and facility letters

(A) APPRAISING A BUSINESS

Introduction

There are always two aspects to business appraisal—financial, and the non-financial matters which are hard to quantify. Whilst the importance of the former is widely accepted and practised, there is a tendency to give scant attention to the latter. This is dangerous because aspects of this general appraisal hold the very key to the success or failure of the business.

General Appraisal

The general appraisal of a business should be concentrated in three main areas:

(a) Markets and products
(b) Resources
(c) Management

(a) Markets and Products

A business fails if it cannot sell its products. The lender needs to be satisfied on the quality of the products and the existence of suitable markets for them. Moreover, all the financial information which a business might provide is dependent on the level of sales. Therefore a lender needs to question a business about its products and markets along the following lines:

Product/services: profitable—unprofitable—details—established—proven—tested—new? Identify markets/segments: growth—decline? Can the total market and market share be quantified? Customers: who are they?—spread?—dominance?

Competition: what is it? What pricing freedom is there?
What are the special skills of the company?
Why should its products/services be bought?
Is there risk from: changing technology—too few customers—special skills, e.g. skilled personnel leaving/retiring—too few suppliers—distribution channels?
How volatile has past demand proved to be?
What is changing? The future will never be the same as the past.
How effective is promotion—advertising—sales?

A lender can learn about markets from a variety of sources. The customer's own research should be made available to supplement the lender's own findings from trade journals, etc. In addition, banks have their own departments which specialise in economic and corporate research.

(b) Resources

In order to carry out its plans, a business must have sufficient production resources. The lender needs to pay particular attention to the following areas:

Premises: location—freehold or leasehold?
               what financial obligations?
               adequacy and suitability?
               valuation and insurance?

Machinery: major items—age—condition—financing?
             what could be sold quickly in a cash crisis—for how much?
             effect of new technology?
             major expenditure last three years—how appraised?
             depreciation policy?
             can planned output be achieved—record of downtime?
             view of efficiency of production processes and controls.

Vehicles: if significant
             age—condition—financing?
             effectiveness of fleet management?
             directors' motor cars—justified?

Labour: assess skills and effectiveness
             problems over quality or availability?
             a fixed or variable cost?
             industrial relations record?

(c) Management

It is often stressed how important it is for a banker to know the customer. This can lead to difficulties however when assessing management capability. The better the customer is known, the more difficult it is to be totally objective. And yet, that is what the lender should try to be. The assessment needs to be based on facts and evidence, not just a subjective personal opinion.

Thus the assessment of management needs to cover the following areas:

Ages—backgrounds—health?
Are there adequate insurance arrangements?
Expertise—sales, production, financial.
Is it weak, lacking in any area? Professional qualifications?

Shareholdings/control—are the managers owners?
Does one man dominate the business? Are responsibilities clearly defined? Is it a balanced team? Management below director level—is there a clear structure? How competent is it?

Track record—what successes and failures have there been and how important were they? Is the past track record relevant to future plans? How committed are they—can they just walk away?

Directors' guarantees?
If the team has been recently formed—is it likely to stick together?
Succession—who will take over when the present directors retire?
Information base for control/decision taking—how good is it and how decisive are they?

A lender will always get a much better 'feel' for a business by visiting the customer's premises. Indeed, in order for an adequate general appraisal of the business to be carried out, it is essential that the lender pays at least one call on the customer, and more if necessary.

Financial Appraisal

Everyone is familiar with what constitutes the financial accounts which a lender examines when assessing a proposition, i.e. balance sheet, profit and loss account and sources and applications of funds statement. Everyone is equally familiar with the limitations of such information, e.g. it is the picture at only one day in the year.

However, such information does provide a valuable starting point for assessing the future possibilities of a business, although it must be remembered that what has happened in the past is not necessarily a guarantee of what is going to happen in the future.

One year's figures are not much use because the lender needs to look at trends. Similarly, one item in a balance sheet (e.g. debtors) cannot tell much in isolation, whereas an examination of debtors, creditors and the run of the bank account, can.

To be of any meaningful use, the accounts need to be received reasonably quickly after the year end, be audited by a reputable firm of accountants and have an auditor's certificate not qualified in any significant way.

The financial appraisal of a business needs to cover three broad areas:

(a) Financial structure
(b) Liquidity
(c) Profitability

(a) Financial Structure

Nearly all businesses are financed by a combination of proprietor's capital and borrowed money (equity and debt). The relationship between the two is very important because a highly geared company (one with a high proportion of debt) is more vulnerable than a lowly geared one.

The financial cost of debt (interest) has to be paid whether or not the company is making profits. This is a particular problem when interest rates are high. The cost of financing equity (dividends) has to be met only out of profits and can, therefore, be waived in difficult times.

A lender is obviously going to be less happy with a highly geared company because of the potential strain placed on it to generate sufficient profits to cover the interest cost.

(i) *Capital Gearing*

The ratio of a company's borrowing to shareholders' funds is called the capital or financial gearing ratio. This can be expressed either gross or net of cash balances. On the basis that cash is readily available to repay borrowing, the net gearing ratio is usually the more significant.

What is an acceptable level of gearing as far as a lender is concerned? Traditionally in the United Kingdom lenders have regarded 100% (1:1) gearing as being the maximum, but very little explanation has been given as to why this should be so. It is sometimes said that a lender does not wish to lend more than the proprietor of a business has injected by way of capital but there are established instances, notably speculative builders, where lenders have always been prepared to see gearing go up to 200% as a normal rule. It is also known that in countries like Germany and Japan, much higher levels of gearing than have been accepted in the United Kingdom have proved tolerable, and in recent years in the United Kingdom successful management buyouts have been arranged with no proprietor's capital at the outset and infinite gearing!

Why can a management buyout with an initial very high level of borrowing and no proprietor's capital turn out to be an acceptable lending proposition? The reason usually is because such propositions have to demonstrate a very strong sustainable cash flow which enables borrowing to be reduced quickly. As has been said above, highly borrowed businesses are vulnerable but those which can generate cash quickly are likely to be less vulnerable than those that cannot.

Cash flow in this context usually means the profit earned on sales. High gearing in a business is unlikely to be acceptable if the business is not able to maintain a satisfactory level of profits under the worst potential market conditions which are likely to exist in the foreseeable future.

Generally speaking a company with a high fixed cost base will see its profits reduce more dramatically should sales fall than one in which costs are variable and fall away with declining sales. Where variable costs account for a large proportion of sales revenue, a business's margin of safety (the margin between its break even point and current, or planned, level of sales) will be wide so that even, say, a 20% drop in sales will still leave a reasonable profit. In such circumstances a highly geared balance sheet may be tolerable.

(ii) *Interest Cover*

It is vital that profit covers the interest on any lending, but the question is: what level represents a suitable degree of safety? A lender should be wary if profit before the deduction of tax and interest does not cover the interest charge at least twice, i.e. if interest is £10,000 then pre-tax, pre-interest profit should be £20,000. It is perhaps not ideal to relate interest cover to historic profits since interest has to be paid out of cash generated from operations. Whilst a business might make profits it may have insufficient cash to pay interest, due to excessive credit terms given to customers, the purchase of fixed assets and so on.

Cashflow is much more volatile than profits and therefore it would be wrong to look at one year's cashflow in isolation. There could, for example, be some extraordinary items of expenditure in one particular year. Instead, a view should be taken over a number of years, as any profitable business would be expected to show a positive cashflow over a longer period.

The cashflow method of calculating interest cover takes the cashflow figure before interest, tax and dividends for at least three years and divides it by interest paid for the same number of years. With this ratio a consistent two times interest cover can be considered to be very satisfactory.

(iii) *Term Debt/Operating Cashflow*

This ratio compares term debt in the balance sheet with operating cashflow taken from the sources and applications of funds statement. The calculation shows the lender how long it will take the company to generate sufficient cash to repay its term debt. Obviously, the shorter the term the better and whilst a long term would not necessarily be alarming, a lender would be looking for something less than two years as being a satisfactory indicator.

(b) Liquidity

The importance of a business's liquidity position cannot be over-stressed because it is an indicator of whether its liabilities can be met when they fall due. Although losses might be the major contributory factor to a business going into liquidation, the real cause will always be a lack of cash.

In simple terms the business must turn its assets into cash at least as quickly as it has to meet its liabilities if it is to avoid borrowing. In most businesses there will be temporary phases when this is not possible and borrowing is the result. Lenders will always be willing to provide facilities to meet temporary shortages of cash provided that they are confident that the business has sufficient capacity to generate cash in the future to repay the lending.

An analysis can be made of the accounts to help reveal the company's past record in respect of liquidity. The appraisal should cover three main areas:

(i)   Assets—how near to cash are they?
(ii) Liabilities—how soon are these due to be paid?
(iii) Funding trends—is the business showing an increasing or lessening need for borrowing?

(i)   *Assets*
When assessing liquidity, it is obviously the current assets which are being examined. Some businesses do have cash and near cash assets such as quoted investments, but in most businesses the current assets are made up of debtors and stock. These can vary in the degree of liquidity they display, and the lender will usually want more information in order to assess how easy they are to turn into cash.

Debtors
1 How well spread are they? A large slow payer or, even worse, a large bad debt could cause real problems.
2 Are debtors increasing out of line with sales? This could indicate a potential bad debt slowing down the overall rate of payment. The average credit given ratio (average debtors ÷ sales × length of accounting period) will reveal any changes in the number of days taken to collect debts.
3 What are the normal credit terms given by the company? Is its relative strength in relation to its customers sufficient to enable it to strictly enforce them?
4 Will the total debtor figure be received in cash from customers or do discounts have to be deducted?
5 Does the company have a history of incurring bad debts?
6 Are any of the debtors located overseas? If so, are the debts insured?

Stock
1 Is stock increasing out of line with sales? The stock turnover ratio (average stock ÷ cost of goods sold × length of accounting period) will show any changes in the number of days taken to turn stock over.
2 How is the stock figure made up? In a company which has raw materials, work-in-progress and finished goods, any changes in the individual levels will affect the real liquidity of the company, i.e. finished goods can be turned into cash more quickly than raw materials in an on-going business.
3 Is the business of a seasonal nature which would make stock holding more or less liquid at different times of the year? Is the balance sheet date at a high or low point in the cycle?

(ii) *Liabilities*
In this analysis, the lender is concerned with those liabilities which have to be satisfied within the forthcoming 12 months, i.e. current liabilities. Again, more information will be required.

Creditors
1 The spread is just as important as it was with debtors. A few large creditors represent potential problems to a business should they start to press for payment. If the company's liquidity position makes it difficult to pay, this could result in delays in the supply of materials.
2 Is the company taking longer to pay? The average credit taken ratio (average creditors ÷ cost of goods sold × length of accounting period) will indicate any changes in the number of days taken to pay creditors.
3 What credit terms are the company able to obtain from suppliers? Is the company managing to pay within those terms?
4 What are the liabilities to preferential creditors? These will rank ahead of a lender if he is unsecured or holds only a floating charge.

Hire Purchase/Leasing
1 What are the repayment terms?
2 Is there evidence of leasing in the balance sheet notes which is not reflected in the figures?

Bank/Short-term Loans/Acceptance Credits
1 Are there other lenders?
2 What are the security arrangements for the facilities?
3 What borrowing facilities are available to the company? How high could gearing go?

Long-term Debt
Only the current portion of any long term debt will be included under the current liabilities heading.
1 Who are the loan creditors?
2 What are the repayment terms?
3 Are the loans secured or unsecured?
4 Is there a facility letter? Are there performance convenants the non-achievement of which may result in the loan being withdrawn?

Inter-company Debt
1 Does this represent an inter-company trading current account position or longer term borrowed money?
2 If the latter, what are the terms of repayment and is interest charged? Is the loan subordinated to outside creditors?
3 Is the debt secured or unsecured?

Loans by Directors
1 What do these amounts represent? Are they actual loans by the directors or are they perhaps undrawn bonuses? Whilst the latter might be viewed favourably, it could also indicate insufficient cash to allow withdrawal.
2 What is the intention in respect of these sums? Do the directors intend to withdraw them in the near future? Alternatively, can the bank regard them as quasi-capital and get the directors to postpone repayment of them?

Dividends
1 Have they been paid to shareholders since the balance sheet date?
2 If payment has not been made, does the company have sufficient cash to pay them and the consequent Advance Corporation Tax?

Taxation
1 Has it been paid since balance sheet date?
2 If not, when is it due and has the company got the cash to meet the obligation?

(iii) *Funding Trends*
An inspection of the statement of Sources and Applications of Funds will enable a lender to identify the movements of cash during the year and ascertain whether there was a net surplus or deficit.

A cash requirement overall is not of itself a bad sign. It may simply represent one year's heavy capital expenditure programme. The trend over a number of years is much more important. Repeated substantial shortages of cash would need to be examined closely as this would seem to suggest a basic weakness in the company if it cannot be self-financing over the longer term.

The particular areas a lender will wish to examine in the Sources and Applications of Funds statement to determine the reasons for a surplus or deficit are:

Working Capital Variation
Working capital needs tend to increase with sales and, in times of high inflation, can increase even on a static real level of sales. The important point is to note how the increase has occurred and whether it can be maintained. It might, for example, be a reflection of overtrading.

Operating Cashflow
Is the company generating sufficient cash to meet all its normal obligations. Even if it does this there still has to be sufficient cash left over to meet loan repayments and the purchase of new fixed assets.

Capital Expenditure
A company's investment in this area needs to be sufficient, otherwise production schedules might not be met. New investment is necessary so that a business keeps pace with the latest technology.

Broadly speaking, capital expenditure should be greater than the depreciation charge to allow for inflation and the higher cost of more technically advanced machinery. However, regard also needs to be given to whether a company could lease rather than buy and allowance has to be made for irregular investment patterns.

It is possible for capital investment to be too high. Future cashflow can be significantly affected by high working capital requirements caused by over investment in areas with low profitability.

As well as looking at the Sources and Applications of Funds statement there are some balance sheet ratios which can also reflect funding trends.

Working Capital Turnover
This ratio (sales ÷ average current assets − average current liabilities) indicates the likely level of working capital needed to finance a certain increase in sales.

A rising trend might point to overtrading, i.e. increasing sales without the provision of the relevant levels of working capital. The adverse effects of this can be avoided in the short term by strict control over debtors, creditors and stock, but the pressures on liquidity will eventually increase to the point where bank finance will be stretched to the limit.

There is no one ratio to be applied across the board—it will vary from industry to industry. For example, it is not uncommon to find food retailers with a negative ratio because their current assets can be sustained at a level less than current liabilities.

Current Ratio

The relationship between current assets and current liabilities shows the availability of short term assets to meet short term liabilities.

Whilst the trend should ideally show an increasing ratio, the type of business involved will affect the lender's opinion of the absolute value. For example, a retailer with cash sales and rapid stock turnover should show a lower ratio than a manufacturer with slow moving stock and a generous credit policy towards customers.

A fall in the ratio might indicate a cut in profit margins, losses, investment of short term funds in fixed assets, or a change in product mix.

Continuous increases in the ratio are not necessarily a good thing. A ratio in excess of two could indicate inefficient use of resources.

Liquid Ratio

This ratio is also known as the 'quick ratio' or the 'acid test'. It differs from the current ratio only in that stock is omitted. It is regarded as being a critical test of a company's real liquidity as only cash or near cash assets are included.

As stock is ignored, a change in the level of stock held giving rise to a corresponding change in creditors, borrowing or cash will have a significant impact on its value.

(c) Profitability

The lender should concentrate on five main aspects of profitability:

1 Are profits increasing with sales?
2 What is the quality of profits? Are they the direct result of trading or is there an extraordinary element in them?
3 Are profits being retained in the business?

4 If a loss has been made, has the cause been identified and remedial action taken?

5 Are there any changes in the return earned on capital employed?

Trends in profitability can be analysed through the examination of a number of ratios.

1 *Profits in Relation to Sales*

The lender will be particularly interested in the margins being achieved and whether they can be sustained and improved upon.

(a) *Gross Margin*

Gross profit as a percentage of sales. It is vital that a reasonable gross margin is maintained if a business is to be profitable since many overheads will be of a fixed or semi-fixed nature.

In most businesses the figure shows the marginal profit to be earned on each £ of sales, and the lender will question any fall seen in the trend. A fall may be a cause for concern, but there may also be acceptable reasons, for example:

(i)   a change in product mix, i.e. higher volume of sales of goods with a lower mark up;

(ii)   reduction of sale price to boost sales volume—this is acceptable provided it works and results in an increased gross profit in overall terms;

(iii) pegging sale price as a result of competition and having to absorb increased prices by suppliers;

(iv)   an increase in any fixed cost elements, e.g. factory rent.

(b) *Net Profit Margin*

Net profit (usually before interest and tax) as a percentage of sales. This shows the performance achieved after deduction of overheads. It is therefore affected not only by changes in demand, production costs, etc., but also by many factors outside the control of the proprietors, e.g. the cost of utilities.

The profit figure before tax and interest should be used in order to ensure that non-trading elements are omitted. Useful comparisons can then be made with other businesses in the same industry to assess the overall performance of the company.

2 *Quality of Profit*

The main concern of a lender, particularly one who lends over a longer term, is to be satisfied that profitability can be sustained over a number of years. Extraordinary profits which occur in any one year need to be discounted, e.g. profits or losses on the sale of fixed assets and losses or gains on foreign exchange. The lender needs to concentrate mainly on trading performance.

The trend in trading performance should be scrutinised. Items such as directors' pension contributions may be discounted as should non-trading income, such as interest on investments.

3 *Retained Profit*

A lender would not expect to see all profits being distributed to shareholders. A business must retain part of its profits to fund future development.

The statement of Sources and Applications of Funds is a useful guide as to whether sufficient funds are being retained. A further rough guide to whether retentions are sufficient to fund increases in sales can be obtained by looking at the relationship between the amount of retentions in relation to sales and the Net Working Assets to Sales ratio as set out below:

$$\frac{\text{Retained profit}}{\text{Sales}}$$ — gives the amount of new capital that a £ of extra sales would produce.

$$\frac{\text{Stock} + \text{Debtors} - \text{Creditors}}{\text{Sales}}$$ — gives the amount of capital that a £ of extra sales would require.

If the second ratio is consistently greater than the first, additional capital, usually in the form of extra borrowing, will be needed to fund expansion.

4 *Losses*

It goes without saying that any lender is going to be concerned when losses appear in a customer's business. For the more serious situations, investigating accountants should be asked to carry out a detailed inspection of the company.

The important aspects of loss making as far as a lender is concerned are:

(a) Are they trading losses or due to extraordinary items?
(b) Can the losses be isolated to particular outlets, branches, activities, contracts, or are they general in nature?
(c) Can the period when they occurred be pin-pointed or are they still occurring?
(d) What action has the company already taken to remedy the situation, and what further action is proposed?

5 *Return on Capital Employed*
This ratio can be applied across the board to all businesses and shows the return enjoyed by the proprietors on their capital investment in the business.

Low returns in the short term may not be critical, but if they persist it would not be logical for the proprietors to continue their investment if it could earn a better return elsewhere.

(B)   CAPITAL INVESTMENT APPRAISAL

The basic object of any investment is that, in return for paying out a given amount of cash today, a larger amount will be received back over a period of time.

A business needs to make careful calculations to ensure that any expenditure is worthwhile, although it has to be said that many companies undertake significant investment projects purely because the management consider them to be 'a good idea'. A lender of funds for capital investment has to be certain that a realistic assessment of the implications of the project has been thoroughly undertaken by the borrower.

Basically, there are four main methods of assessing capital investment projects:

(a) Payback—this involves the calculation of the time it will take to recover the initial outlay.
(b) Return on investment—this indicates the average annual percentage return on either the average or alternatively the total amount of the investment.
(c) Net present value return on investment—this method involves the discounting of future cash inflows from the project. It adjusts the return to allow for the time value of money (cash received now is more valuable than cash received in the future because it can be invested to earn an income in the intervening period).
(d) Yield (or internal rate of return)—this method uses the same principles as the net present value approach but with the objective of establishing the discount rate at which the present values of the cash inflows and outflows match.

Each method has its merits but it is widely accepted that the most accurate assessments of the return from an investment project are provided by the methods which involve the discounting of cashflows. However, whichever approach is adopted, the results for the appraisal have to be critically assessed, as follows:

(a) How good is the management at investment appraisal? Have previous appraisals been accurate?

(b) Is the objective of the investment and the method of appraisal realistic?

(c) What assumptions have been made concerning the amount and timing of future revenues, in particular those to be received in the immediate future as this tends to be the more critical period.

(d) Have any sensitivity tests been carried out, e.g. what would the position be if sales were 20% less than forecast or interest rates 2% higher?

(e) Will the project affect the business in other respects, e.g. will extra working capital be required?

(f) Have all costs been included, e.g. has allowance been made for extra skilled labour or training existing staff?

(g) Are the costs of the project subject to increases, e.g. because machinery has to be imported from abroad and paid for in foreign currency?

(h) Could delays in deliveries seriously affect the calculations?

(i) Will full production be possible immediately or does allowance need to be made for an initial delay?

(C) APPRAISING PROFITABILITY FORECASTS

Introduction

A company's plans in relation to its trading activities need to be incorporated in an operating budget, which should cover at least the next 12 months. Ideally, the operating budget should represent the current year portion of a longer term financial plan.

The management should not only be committed to meeting their budgeted figures, but should be prepared to use them as a means of controlling and monitoring their business. A lender should always be wary of any budget which appears to have been put together solely because he asked for it.

Many assumptions and estimates will have been made by the company in drawing up their plan, and the validity of these will determine the accuracy of the budget. The appraisal of budgets should involve the identification of significant items and questioning the management to ensure the underlying assumptions are soundly based.

The following is a suggested list of items which the lender might question:

General Points

— Which individual factor would be most likely to result in the company not being able to achieve its forecast?
— How will the company be affected by economic conditions and cyclical trends?
— Has the effect of inflation been considered in drawing up the estimates?
— Are the forecasts reasonable in relation to last year's actual results?
— How accurate have previous forecasts been?

Sales

— What does the forward order book look like?
— Does the company have a good spread of products and customers, or is it reliant on only one?
— Does the company give discounts and have these been allowed for in the sales forecast?
— Are the sales figures exclusive or inclusive of VAT?
— Are the company's forecasts based on existing markets or do they require the opening up of new markets?
— Has any research been undertaken?
— Are sales going to be affected by technological changes, and if so, when?
— Does the company have any exposure to exchange rate risks?
— Are sales seasonal and, if so, has allowance been made?
— Are forecast sales dependent upon new plant and machinery being installed and, if so, when might this occur?
— Has allowance been made for possible bad debts?

Materials

— What materials are needed and when? How does this relate to budgeted sales?
— How have the costs of materials been calculated?
— Are raw materials readily available and what assumptions about delivery times have been made?
— What estimates have been made about stock levels?
— Is the company stocking up or de-stocking?
— Has the impact of discounts been allowed for; both trade discounts and possible discounts on bulk orders?
— What allowances have been made for wastage and losses on scrap?
— Does the company need to sub-contract? If so, do they have alternative sources of supply if necessary?

— Has the exchange risk been covered on imports purchased in foreign currency?

Labour

— Has any allowance been made for increases in the wage bill? There will usually be an annual wage increase.
— Has training been budgeted for, and the impact of starters and leavers generally?
— Does the company have sufficient skilled labour?
— Have all labour costs been included, e.g. National Insurance contributions, pensions, etc.?
— Will overtime be necessary? Has the extra cost been estimated and included?

Expenses

— Have all expenses been included?

Direct Wages	Indirect Wages	Rent
Salaries	Rates	Insurance
Fees	Electricity	Overtime premium
Gas	Holiday Pay	Printing
National Insurance	Stationery	Postage
Materials	Telephone	Loose tools
Legal Fees	Consumable stores	Audit fees
Water Rates	Finance charges	Bank charges
Maintenance	Canteen expenses	Sub-contractors
Packing	Bought-in-components	Transport
Depreciation	Selling commission	Cash discounts
Publicity	Bad debts	Travelling
Entertaining	Research & Dev.	Pensions

— Are the significant items realistic?
— Has director's remuneration been included?
— Has allowance been made for the extra interest charge on any increased levels of borrowing which are anticipated?
— Is the interest rate used in the budgets realistic?

Budgeted figures should be allocated to the month in which they are expected to occur, but an annual total should also be shown. This can then be compared with the last audited accounts and large differences questioned.

A lender should always treat with caution forecasts which are significantly different to the previous year's actual figures.

Forecasts will always contain elements of significant uncertainty, and as part of his analysis the lender should carry out some tests to see how sensitive the budgets are to changes in these uncertain areas. 'What if' questions need to be asked about those factors which are least easy to predict and/or are likely to have the most impact on profits.

The ready availability of personal computers makes such sensitivity analyses a more simple task than in the past. However, as an alternative, break even analysis can be used. This analysis revolves around the cost/volume/profit relationship within a business and can be used to show the effects of price reduction/increases and changes in different types of cost on profits.

Any significant variance in actual figures from those budgeted will bring the figures for the rest of the period into question. Where it becomes apparent that plans have gone significantly awry, an updated budget should be sought.

(D)   APPRAISING LIQUIDITY FORECASTS

Budgets can be translated into a cashflow forecast which, by taking into account the timing of cash inflows and outflows, shows a company's funding needs. The cashflow forecast will make due allowance for credit given and taken when estimating receipts and payments. The lender will want to see both the cashflow forecast and the operating and capital expenditure budgets on which it will be based.

Lenders are often offered cashflow forecasts without accompanying budgets. Whilst it is not impossible to draw the cashflow forecast without first producing a budget, it has to be based on the sort of assumptions which are normally incorporated into budgets, and if the lender does receive such a forecast he will need to test it with the sort of questions set out in the previous section.

In addition there will be questions solely relating to the cashflow forecast itself:

(a) Does the period between sales and payment reflect collection experience and not just terms of trade?
(b) Has VAT been correctly dealt with in the forecast?
(c) Have non profit and loss items such as capital expenditure and loan repayments been included?
(d) Have non-cash costs such as depreciation been excluded?

(e) Do receipts and payments generated by sales and expenditure in the previous period correspond with the end of period debtors and creditors?

(f) The forecast only usually shows the cash position at the end of each month, i.e. the net effect of inflows and outflows during the month. Can the company forecast the maximum requirement during each month?

(g) Does the starting point look realistic, e.g. is the opening bank balance right?

If the lender is doubtful about the assumptions on which the forecast is based then, as with budgets, sensitivity tests should be carried out, for example looking at the cash requirement if debtors take longer to pay.

The information from the cashflow forecast and the operating and capital expenditure budgets will allow a projected balance sheet to be drawn up as well as a statement of Sources and Applications of Funds. The lender will then be in a position to check these against the latest historical figures. Ratios can be projected to show the future position of the company and the lender will then be in a position to decide whether, say, the anticipated level of gearing is going to be acceptable.

(E)   MONITORING AND CONTROL

Introduction

This is an area to which many lenders pay too little attention but, if it is carried out properly, the incidence of a lender's losses due to bad debts can be greatly reduced.

All lending contains an element of risk, and the main risk areas for a particular business need to be identified as part of the initial appraisal. The lender can then focus on these in the monitoring process. Examples of weakness might be the inability to achieve budgeted sales or profit margins and the lender's monitoring system should enable him to pick up such trends at an early stage.

The bank lender has a number of aids to assist in monitoring his customer:

(a) Internal records
(b) Visits and interviews
(c) Audited accounts
(d) Management accounts.

Internal Records

Lenders will be able to call upon their own computerised reporting systems to provide information which will enable a company's sales and liquidity to be monitored. For example, turnover through a bank account will give a reasonable indicator of the level of sales. For those companies which provide little or no management information, internal records are the only way in which effective monitoring can be carried out.

The two main types of computer report which banks use are:

(a) a daily reference list
(b) a summary of account information and trends.

(a)   Daily Reference List

This report informs the lender when a customer is exceeding the agreed limit or goes overdrawn without arrangement. Obviously excesses need to be questioned. It may be that the lender will be prepared to mark an increased overdraft limit, however if this is not the case a complete review of lending needs to be undertaken with the customer.

(b)   Summary of Account Information and Trends

These reports show the historical run of a business's bank account and provide a good means for judging liquidity trends. The areas which need to be examined are:

(i)   What is the highest debit balance trend?
(ii)   What is the lowest debit balance trend? Does the account swing into credit or is a hardcore developing? Is any hardcore increasing in size?
(iii) Is there any deterioration in the average balance?
(iv)   How does the debit turnover compare with sales? If it is out of line it might indicate the existence of an account with another bank.
(v)   Is the general pattern of the account changing? Is seasonal borrowing being taken earlier? Are reductions coming later or not at all?

Where a business gives cause for concern it is vital that frequent information is obtained on at least a monthly basis so that worrying trends are taken up with the customer without delay.

Visits and Interviews

Whilst statistical information obtained from the bank account and other records can be useful, a visit to a customer's premises is usually essential, for the following reasons:

(a) It gives the lender a 'feel' of the actual business represented by the figures.
(b) It shows an interest in the business which is appreciated by the customer.
(c) The customer will be more willing to talk fully about his business on 'home ground'.
(d) It gives an opportunity to meet all the management team rather than just the ones who deal with finance.
(e) It allows an impression to be formed of the organisation of the business.

Visiting should not be undertaken haphazardly. The lender should have a programmed schedule but obviously the number of visits made will vary according to the circumstances. An occasional brief social call is usually welcome as an addition to the more formal occasions when, for example, the lending is being reviewed.

For troublesome customers, an unannounced visit can be very revealing.

The key to a successful visit or interview is good preparation. The lender needs clear objectives and some sort of agenda of discussion points is essential, e.g. assessment of actual performance to date compared to budget and alterations to future plans.

Audited Accounts

The ideal time to review lending is when the audited accounts become available.

Whilst audited accounts are a useful tool for monitoring progress, they can vary very much in quality. Much will depend on the auditors and their relationship with their client. Theoretically, of course, the accounts represent an independent view of the business. Practically, this is often not the case. The auditors' approach is going to be different in those businesses where there are outside shareholders compared to companies where the directors own all the shares. In the latter case, the auditors' main concern will probably be to minimise the business's tax burden.

Ideally, a lender would like to see accounts audited by one of the major partnerships. Small firms of accountants, whilst probably being more than capable, are more likely to produce figures which satisfy their client's particular wishes because they cannot afford to sacrifice the fees the relationship generates.

It is always useful to compare audited figures with any management figures which might have been produced. The level of accuracy of the management figures will give the lender a useful guide as to the extent to which reliance can be placed on future figures.

Management Accounts

A lender will require regular figures in order to check actual results against budgeted projections. The monitoring of management accounts gives an early warning of problems and enables a reasonable prediction to be made of what might happen.

A major benefit of management accounts is the opportunity they give to the lender to see how the assumptions made in the budget are working in reality. The capacity to repay borrowing is going to be seriously impaired by such things as lower levels of sales, tighter margins or a bad debt. Where actual performance is significantly different to budgets, the whole situation needs to be reviewed with new forecasts being produced. If the management of the company is doing its job, it will be revising its plans without any prompting from the lender.

For most businesses, the level of sales will be the most fundamental assumption in their budgeting. Particular attention should therefore be given by the lender to monitoring sales performance. The following comparisons of sales should be made:

(a) actual monthly sales against forecast;
(b) cumulative figures to date for actual and forecast sales;
(c) with the previous year's actual.

Not too much attention should be paid to a poor performance in any individual month because the position might be corrected later. It is the cumulative total which is more important. The company's order book should also be scrutinised where manufacturing to order is an important element of sales. A lack of orders will be a warning sign.

It is not difficult for a business to show a more favourable position than exists in reality, simply by adjusting the stock figure. The lender has to some extent to take the management accounts on trust but, if doubts arise, then an auditor's confirmation of the management accounts should be insisted upon.

(F)   MEDIUM TERM LENDING AND FACILITY LETTERS

Short term lending is repayable on demand or within 12 months, whereas repayment of medium term lending is scheduled over a predetermined period.

Obviously it is much easier to predict what might happen over a short period than it is over a period of 10 years or more. Repayment of short term lending can be assessed more accurately from reasonably certain cashflows over the next 12 months, but this is not so for longer term lending.

Over the longer term the fundamental strength of the company and the capability of its management become much more important matters. Its products need to be of good quality and the future of its markets stable. The company's planning needs to be realistic as must be its capacity to obtain the resources to achieve its objectives.

Unlike an overdraft for which demand can be made at any time, a medium term loan will be subject to the formal documentation of a facility letter laying out a set of conditions. Demand for repayment will only usually be possible on breach of one or more of those conditions.

With term lending, there is a longer period during which the company's fortunes can change. To protect itself against adverse changes, a bank builds into its facility letter covenants with which the borrower has to comply. Failure to comply will give the bank the right to demand repayment or to re-negotiate the loan. The main purpose of covenants is to ensure that the business maintains sufficient financial strength, particularly adequate liquidity, to enable it to service the bank's loan and its other commitments. Covenants will often lay down a rigid set of performance standards and customer resistance to them is by no means uncommon.

The number and severity of the covenants will depend on the circumstances. Where a lender has doubts about a company's ability to sustain sufficient liquidity over a longer period, he is likely to demand a higher level of safeguards. This is especially likely where a borrower might fall into one of the following categories:

(a)   The borrower is highly geared.
(b)   The profit record is unimpressive.
(c)   The borrower is trying to take over a business which is bigger than itself, or one whose activities are completely different.
(d)   The company has access to several lines of credit from other lenders which, if fully utilised, could make the level of gearing unacceptable, and could adversely affect profitability.

There are a very wide range of covenants which can be obtained from borrowers. Some might be specifically tailored to cover particular circumstances, but the most typical covenants are:

(a) Negative pledge—an agreement not to give security to other lenders. This is most obviously necessary where a borrower is multi-banked.
(b) Gearing restriction—the lender places a limit on the amount the customer can borrow in relation to net worth.
(c) Minimum level for net tangible assets—this provides protection against losses or reduction in capital or reserves as a result of asset write-offs.
(d) Interest cover—a formula will be included under which interest will have to be covered by pre-tax, pre-interest profit on an agreed multiplier. Two times cover is the usual minimum.
(e) Change of ownership—this covenant ensures that control of the company will not change hands, and is particularly important where the company is part of a larger group.

The extent of covenants has to be realistic in relation to the borrower's size and circumstances. Sometimes a lender has to accept a less than ideal level of covenants and, in those situations, it would be possible to agree a formula whereby the covenanted performance standards are increased over time.

8 CORPORATE LENDING AND SECURITY

This chapter concentrates on the value of corporate security and the problems associated with it. It is not intended to deal with the technicalities of charging security which are well covered in other books. Security will be examined under the following headings:

(a) When should security be taken?
(b) Security margins
(c) Property valuation
(d) Occupational leases
(e) Second mortgages
(f) Debentures
(g) Guarantees and other third party security
(h) Letters of Comfort.

(A) WHEN SHOULD SECURITY BE TAKEN?

The main considerations are the same as for personal borrowers.
    A lender should consider taking security in the following situations:

(a) Where the realisation of specific assets represents the source of repayment, e.g. a bridging loan.
(b) Where the purpose of the advance is to acquire a specific asset, e.g. a medium term loan for the purchase of machinery.
(c) Where the risks and consequences of the expected source of repayment failing are such as to make it necessary to have a clearly defined and controlled alternative source.

The circumstances in which the first two situations will arise are obvious. Most difficulties will be found in assessing the third and it is this area which will be considered in detail. The evaluation can be split into two parts:

(a) The risks—the likelihood of the expected source of repayment breaking down.

(b) The consequences—if the primary source of repayment did fail, would the lender obtain clearance of the borrowing if control over, and the power to sell, specific assets was not held?

A practical approach is needed and the lender should be 'amount conscious'. It will not be cost effective to take security for small sums, nor should items be charged which are difficult to control, value or realise (e.g. jewellery, antiques, etc.).

The basic approach is the same as for personal borrowers but the process of assessment will be more complex.

Risks

In analysing the risk of repayment breakdown, the following factors should be considered:

(a) The track record of the business—budgets and forecasts must be assessed alongside the historical figures and the assumptions under which they have been produced questioned, especially where significant improvements on past performance are being projected.
(b) Supporting evidence—what proportion of sales is based on definite orders? Are there any increases in costs in the pipeline?
(c) Sensitivity analysis—the 'what if' questions. What would be the effect on the business if sales are 25% less than budget or if costs increase by 10% more than forecast? The vulnerability of the business to small changes in its trading circumstances needs to be tested.
(d) Gearing—companies with a high level of borrowing in relation to net worth may have to apportion a significant part of net income to pay interest. Generally speaking, lenders need to look carefully where capital gearing is above 70% and/or interest cover below three times.
(e) Quality of management—how reliable are management forecasts? Does actual performance usually match projections? The lender's view of management should be based on evidence, not opinion. Is the business too dependent on one person? If so life cover should be considered.

Consequences

If a business is unable to repay its debts, the eventual consequence will be a winding up or liquidation. To assess the outcome of this event, it will be necessary to carry out a break-up analysis of the balance sheet. This will give a significantly different picture to the balance sheet as a going concern for the following reasons:

(a) Assets lose value as soon as trading ceases, and some may have no value at all, for example, work in progress. Asset values have to be discounted. The discount factors to be applied will vary from business to business and some commonsense reasoning needs to be applied to individual assets. For example, a stock of high fashion clothing which has not sold is unlikely to be worth very much. Similarly, debtors in contracting businesses— where counter claims for breach of contract could be made— may produce a low realisation.

Average realisation figures have to be treated with some caution but in recent years these have probably been in the order of the following percentages of book values:

Freehold and leasehold land and buildings 40%
Finished goods stock   25%–30%
Debtors   65%–75%

The surprise to most lenders is that property realisations are so far below book value, but there are good reasons why this should be so and which give an illustration of how discount factors have to be arrived at:

(i) The book figure is probably historical cost. There is no reason why price should necessarily equal or exceed cost in a forced sale.

(ii) If the book figure is a valuation it may not be on an open market basis. Many directors' valuations are based on an existing use value which may not be appropriate when a business has failed.

Even a professional valuation might have been made on a similar basis and was perhaps carried out when market conditions were different. In practice, it is difficult for a meaningful forced sale valuation to be established because it is impossible to predict the conditions under which the forced sale will be made necessary.

(iii) An effective market for the type of property might have ceased to exist, either because of a general recession or one in a particular industry or area.

(iv) The figures will include some short leases where a particularly poor level of realisation is to be expected.

(b) The lender will rank behind preferential creditors and other lenders who have taken security. The liquidation will occur in the future, probably following significant losses, so that the business's net assets will be less than at present.

An unsecured lender ranks equally with other unsecured creditors. An analysis of the break-up value of the balance sheet might show that on winding up there would only be a small surplus for unsecured creditors or even a shortfall. If that is the case, the lender must consider taking security where the risks of repayment breakdown are significant or are difficult to assess.

(B) SECURITY MARGINS

The most common form of tangible security taken for business propositions are:

(a) Land and property
(b) Debentures.

The problems involved in valuing debentures and establishing debenture formulae are examined later in this chapter. This section will concentrate on the extent of the security margins needed on property if a lender requires security realisation to repay an advance in full.

Why is a Margin Needed?

If a lending of 100% of security valuation is made, the realisation proceeds from the sale of the assets will not repay the full borrowing because it will not cover:

(a) Any fall in value between the date of the advance and the sale of the asset. So with a long term lending, the uncertainty of realisable value may be greater and therefore a wider margin may be needed.
(b) The costs of sale and other necessary costs relating to the need to keep the asset saleable, such as security, insurance and maintenance costs on a property.
(c) The roll up of interest since the last charging date.

For a lender to be fully secured, the security margin should include a reasonable estimate of the effect of these elements on the security value. The absence of an adequate margin means that the advance may not be fully repaid from the sale of the security and it needs to be recognised that such a lending is, in reality, only partially secured, even though the face value of the security is greater than the lending.

Land and Property

Most professional property valuations are based on an open market value at the time of the valuation. This assumes a willing buyer and seller, and a reasonable period for the sale to be negotiated taking into account the nature of the property and the state of the market. Estimates of selling and legal fees can easily be obtained from local estate agents and solicitors, whilst 12 months would be a prudent assumption in respect of interest roll up. The main problem with the property will lie in translating its present open market value into a future forced sale value. This will be a subjective judgment influenced by the type, location, age, quality and condition of the property.

Commercial property has a more narrow market than residential property and therefore presents more difficulties. Commercial properties represent good security when occupied and when future prospects of occupation are good. But security is not needed to cover the good times and the same properties may become poor security when they are vacant and there is no buyer. The sort of properties which are likely to give the greatest problems are those which are older or of a specialised nature. Such properties can be subject to a very severe discount on a forced sale and it would probably not be prudent to lend more than 30% of open market valuation. Even with some of the best properties, a lending of more than 60% of open market value may carry a risk of not achieving full recovery on a forced sale.

These percentages might appear low but a simple illustration based on general experience will show why they are realistic.

Assuming that in a good location it will take a year for the sale of a commercial property to be completed (by no means an unusual occurrence) and that a price reduction of 20% may be required from open market valuation, the need for a high security margin becomes obvious:

5%-7%	— to cover agent's fees, legal expenses, etc.
12%-15%	— interest roll up for one year
20%	— reduction in price
say, 40%	

Any less favourable conditions than those above (e.g. if longer than a year is taken to sell) will necessitate an even higher margin to ensure full security cover.

(C) PROPERTY VALUATION

Lenders are not expert property valuers and cannot view a property with the skill of the professional valuer. Some properties are difficult to value because of their specialised nature or location, and others might require a detailed internal inspection.

Lenders are sometimes tempted to put a 'ball park' valuation on a property, particularly when the borrower resists paying the cost of a professional valuation. Such an approach may be satisfactory when lending only a small amount but when the security is being relied on for a significant sum, the services of a professional valuer are essential.

Renewal of Valuations

Under normal circumstances it is prudent to re-value security every three years, although there will be occasions where it should be done more frequently. This would usually be required when the lender's risk was high.

By the same token, if a lending is being repaid satisfactorily or if security is relied on for only a small proportion of its value, revaluation can be dispensed with unless the area in which the property is located is showing a serious decline in property values generally.

(D) OCCUPATIONAL LEASES

An occupational lease is generally defined as a tenancy agreement, usually for a term of less than 30 years. The occupation of property is obtained in consideration of a rent payment which is subject to regular reviews usually at three, five or seven-year intervals.

Many small businesses and shops operate from premises on the basis of such short tenancies. Only rarely will an occupational lease represent good security. Although they often have an open market value, it is unusual for them to have a forced sale value. The reasons for this are:

(a) The lease is likely to contain a bankruptcy clause, whereby it is forfeit if the lessee goes bankrupt or into liquidation—the precise occasion when a lender would be looking to sell the security.

(b) The lease will be forefeit if the rent is not paid but it is not usually worthwhile for a lender to fund rent payments merely in order to retain the security. This is because any profit rental which you will accrue between rent reviews will be eliminated at the next review. The consequence is that the value of the lease will usually be low compared with the annual rental payments—it might even be below the rent figure. It would not, therefore, be sensible to meet, say, one or two quarters' rent to preserve the security unless there were very positive reasons for believing an early sale of the lease could be achieved.

The most prudent view to take of occupational leases is to regard them as having no security value at all. Despite this, a lender with a charge over such a lease does have control over what is usually the major asset in a small business. This means that the business cannot be disposed of without the borrowing being repaid and for this reason it is usually advisable for a lender to take a charge on an occupational lease even though the security value will be nil.

(E)   SECOND MORTGAGES

Second and subsequent mortgages over land are some of the most common forms of security taken by lending institutions. There is a tendency to regard all second charges as being of a similar quality but this is incorrect as some represent better security than others.

Value of Equity

Of crucial importance when assessing the value of a second charge, is the relationship between the amount of the prior charges and the size of the equity available to the lender.

In order to realise the security, a lender would have to pay off prior mortgages. The more usual alternative is that the lender sits tight and waits for the first mortgagee to sell the property—presuming their loan is not being repaid either. The disadvantage of this alternative is that whilst the first mortgagee is obliged to get the best price possible for the property, his prime concern will be to obtain repayment of his own debt, not that of subsequent mortgagees.

Earlier in this chapter, the size of the security margin necessary on property was discussed. In order for a second or subsequent mortgage to fully secure a borrowing, a larger margin will be needed than where a first charge is concerned. It has to be remembered that it would be the second mortgagee's equity which would bear the brunt of any reduction in the value of the property and/or the roll up of interest (on all mortgages—not just the lender's own). Where the total of prior mortgages exceeds the recommended proportions of valuation set out in paragraph (B), Security Margins, the lender should regard the second charge as being of minimal value only.

However, the lender's position is much stronger where prior

mortgages are small in relation to the overall property value. A lender may be willing to repay a small first mortgage in order to control a forced sale and an acceptable security margin is much more likely to be achieved.

Matrimonial Homes

Special problems can be posed when matrimonial homes are taken as security, especially where the borrowing to be secured is not directly related to the purchase or improvement of the property. This is because the mortgagor may be reluctant to sacrifice the family home to see a lender repaid following failure of his or her business.

It is not prudent to lend against a second or subsequent mortgage on a matrimonial home to an extent where the mortgagor would lose everything if the lender realised the security. A larger margin than the 20% mentioned in relation to residential property should be considered so that, if things go wrong, the mortgagor will still have some cash left over to put down as a deposit on a new property, following the sale of the old one. It is good policy to leave the borrower some room to start again as this will make the realisation of security a much less painful business all round.

(F) DEBENTURES

This section concentrates on the valuation and monitoring of debenture security.

Priority in Winding Up

Holding a debenture as security improves a lender's position in a winding up in relation to the other creditors. In a company winding up, the priority of payments from asset sales is as follows:

(a) The expenses of winding up
(b) Holders of a fixed charge over those assets
(c) Preferential creditors
(d) Holders of a floating charge
(e) Unsecured creditors
(f) Shareholders

Nature of the Security

The most common form of bank debenture now provides the following security:

(a) A legal fixed first charge on freehold and leasehold property whether registered or unregistered title, together with building fixtures, including trade fixtures and fixed plant and machinery.

   The definition of fixed plant means machinery fixed to the floor. This should not be confused with the accountancy definition of fixed assets, which will include moveable assets such as vehicles, which would not be covered by the debenture's fixed charge.

(b) An equitable fixed first charge on all future freehold or leasehold property, together with building fixtures including trade fixtures and fixed plant and machinery.

(c) An equitable fixed first charge over all book debts and other debts now and from time to time owing, and over goodwill and uncalled capital.

(d) A first floating charge over all other assets whatsoever both present and future. The principal assets remaining to be caught under the floating charge are stock, moveable plant and machinery and motor vehicles.

Doubt often exists as to whether plant and machinery is covered by the fixed or floating element of a debenture. Where such assets are of significant value, the lender has the option of taking a separate Chattel Mortgage which will provide a fixed charge over a particular asset.

A floating charge will not cover borrowing which was taken before the date of the debenture unless either the hardening period has expired, or it can be proved that the company was solvent at the time the debenture was taken.

The hardening period can be defined most simply as:

(a) either, at worst, the 12 month period following the creation of the debenture (this would usually relate to loan accounts)

(b) or, the time taken for the debit balance on the day the debenture was taken to be turned over by subsequent credits—this would usually be relevant when an overdraft is being secured. This is an instance where Clayton's case works in the lender's favour.

Simple Floating Charges

Prior to the passing of the 1986 Insolvency Act, lenders were able to appoint a Law of Property Act Receiver to safeguard their interests when they had a charge over fixed property. The provisions of the Insolvency Act allowed any creditor to appoint an Administrator to take control of the property and such an Administrator would rank ahead of a Law of Property Act Receiver. It was perceived by many lending institutions that an Administrator appointed by creditors might act in a way to prejudice the value of the lender's security.

A Receiver appointed under a floating charge takes precedence over an Administrator and for this reason some lenders have drawn up simple forms of debenture comprising a simple floating charge incorporating the right to appoint a Receiver. These simple forms of debenture are not usually intended to be regarded as security— a normal bank debenture would be taken if this was necessary— but merely as a way of being able to appoint a Receiver under a floating charge and thereby putting the lender back in the position that existed before the passing of the Insolvency Act.

Simple debentures are mainly used for property or building advances where the only security would usually be a charge over the property and the lender would not wish any other party to gain control of it.

Valuing the Debenture

The security value of a debenture is the amount which would be realised on Receivership or winding up less any priority claims.

Prior Claims

The three principal claims which have priority over a debenture holder are:

1   *Receivership costs*—the fees of the Receiver are negotiable depending on the complexity of the Receivership. Whilst the more complex Receiverships might result in fees in excess of 10% of asset realisations, the average will usually be around 5%.

2   *Preferential creditors*—these have priority over a floating charge. A full list of preferential creditors can be found in Schedule 6 of the Insolvency Act 1986, but the major items are:

   (a)   VAT for six months
   (b)   PAYE, Social Security contributions, Betting Duty, etc.— for 12 months
   (c)   wages, holiday pay, etc., due to employees
   (d)   contributions to occupational pension schemes.

(Rates and Corporation Tax are no longer preferential following the introduction of the Insolvency Act).

Preferential creditors tend to increase substantially when a business is in trouble because the company will defer payment of VAT, PAYE, etc., in order to maintain reasonable relations with the creditors on which it is dependent for supply of components, raw materials, etc.

Crown monies due to companies can be set off against VAT and PAYE monies owing. Although this right falls into something of a grey area, it needs to be recognised that the power ostensibly exists.

3   *Retention of title*—Romalpa clauses entitle a supplier to retain title to goods supplied until payment is received. Retention of title clauses can be drawn up in many different ways but they will usually seek to cover both stock and debtors.

It is not easy to establish the full extent to which assets are subject to retention of title because borrowers tend to take little notice of it. It is not something which has practical relevance to the day to day management of their business and they will usually not even know where to look in the range of documentation from their supplier to establish whether such clauses exist. A lender therefore needs to be circumspect in accepting the borrower's assessments of the extent of retention of title. It is imperative that, if stock and debtors form a significant part of the security, the lender should seek copies of the conditions of sale imposed by suppliers. The relevant clauses may appear on the back of invoices or be documented separately.

Romalpa clauses are now so prevalent that it may not always be practical to carry out a full check where a large number of suppliers is involved. In such situations, the most prudent course may be to assume that all raw material stock not paid for is subject to retention of title.

The position in respect of work in progress, finished goods and debtors is not so clear. In order to enforce a retention of title clause, the goods and proceeds must be separately identifiable as belonging to the supplier. This will be made more difficult as manufacturing takes place and the supplier's goods become inextricably mixed with other materials.

The situation regarding Romalpa clauses over debtors is even more unclear. At the time of writing there is no legal case law and it does not appear that a supplier has yet been successful in enforcing a claim which runs through to debtors. The area of most potential danger seems to lie where the goods remain readily identifiable whilst passing through the borrower's hands to his debtor. Wholesaling type businesses may therefore be particularly vulnerable.

Establishing Asset Realisation Values

It is not possible to standardise the discount factors to be applied to the book values of assets because they will vary with the nature of the assets and the type of business. Nevertheless, book values must be discounted and the following general guidelines are based on average realisations from recent receiverships and liquidations:

1   Land and buildings. This subject was covered in detail in the section on Security Margins.
2   Plant and machinery. Realisation values are usually considerably below book values—averaging 20/25%. Older machinery may have no more than scrap value, whilst specialist machinery will attract only a limited market. Some items, notably machinery in the printing industry, hold their value, as do motor vehicles.

   It is probably wise to seek a professional valuation in those cases where plant and machinery represent a significant part of the security, and particularly where a specific Chattel Mortgage has been taken.
3   Debtors. Realisation will usually only be around 65-75% of book value. The reasons for this will include:

   (a)   Doubtful and irrecoverable debts, including inter-group debtors.
   (b)   Breach of contract claims. This will be particularly relevant to companies involved in long term contracts (e.g. the construction industry) and companies which offer after sales service contracts. Banks are generally reluctant to advance further monies to a Receiver in order that contracts can be completed.
   (c)   Counter claims by debtors for money owed to them.
   (d)   Claims that the quality of goods or services supplied is sub-standard.
   (e)   Attempts, mainly by small debtors, to avoid payment in the hope that the Receiver will regard their recovery as not being time or cost effective.

   The size of the discount factor applied to a company's debtors will be based on the extent to which the above points apply.
4   Stock. Realisations are generally very poor at 10-20% of book value, the reasons being:

   (a)   finished goods being out of date or unsaleable;
   (b)   work in progress having to be discontinued;
   (c)   raw materials being subject to retention of title.

Example of Debenture Valuation

The following example is based on a real and typical case and shows the impact of applying discount factors to book values.

Assets pledged under floating charge	Book Value £000	Realisation %	Estimated to realise £000
Stock	400	15	60
Plant, Vehicles & Equipment	240	30	72
	640		132

Assets pledged under fixed charge			
Freehold & Leasehold Premises	800	40	320
Debtors	600	67	400
Fixed Plant & Equipment	280	20	56
	2320		776
Due to Bank	1000		
add cost of receivership (5% of realisations)	46		1046
Deficiency under fixed charge			(270)
Preferential creditors			
— PAYE/NI			40
— VAT			150
— Holiday pay			10
— Employees			40 240
Deficiency after preferential claims			(108)
Deficiency as regard debenture holder			(270)

In this example a loss of £270,000 was incurred despite apparently being more than twice covered by total assets on book values. It illustrates two important lessons:

(a) A floating charge often has only limited value.
(b) The need for a strong debenture formula if full security cover is required.

Setting Debenture Formulae

The two main reasons for setting debenture formulae are:

1   to establish an adequate security margin;
2   to create a warning system to trigger investigation.

The lender does not in fact set the formula, it sets itself. It has to reflect the company's projected future assets in relation to anticipated borrowing, and will be determined therefore by the company's future budgets. The question for the lender will be whether the achievable formula represents an adequate level of security cover.

The relationship between the assets and borrowing which the lender seeks to monitor is that shown in the company's books. The formula should therefore be related to the bank balance in the company's books and not that which appears on bank statements (which will not reflect cheques issued but not presented).

If a lending is to be fully secured, the valuation of the debenture must show a surplus and continue to do so in the future. Since the expectation of realisations from a floating charge is generally poor, the cover provided by the fixed charge is crucial. Part of the lending might be covered by the value of property and fixed plant and machinery, but in the main the lender will be looking to the fixed charge over book debts. With average debtor realisations at around 67%, the minimum acceptable formula will usually be $1\frac{1}{2}$ times the liabilities to be covered. A higher multiple will be needed in those businesses where a poor level of debt recovery is seen, such as clothing and contracting.

The formula should exclude long standing debtors (over 90 days in most businesses) as these may be of doubtful quality. Debts due from companies in the same group or associated companies should similarly be omitted.

Usually the overall current asset multiple in the formula will not be as important as the debtor element. Nevertheless, a current asset multiple will ensure that the lending finances assets as opposed to reducing creditors. Thus the number of times current assets should cover borrowing will be of more use as a monitoring tool than as a reflection of security value.

Where stock represents a major part of the security value, those elements covered by retention of title and work in progress should not be included and a high multiple, at least three times, should be set.

In those cases where it is not possible to achieve a satisfactory debenture formula, for example where only once debtor cover is available, the lending will only be partially secured and the risk will have to be addressed accordingly.

Monitoring and Evaluating Debenture Figures

In all but exceptional cases, where a debenture is being taken as security, a formula should be agreed with the borrower. The agreement should stipulate the monitoring information to be supplied and the frequency and timescale for receipt. Monthly monitoring should be the norm with information being received not more than three weeks following the date of the figures.

In order to impress on the customer how important the information is, it is good practice to acknowledge receipt of the figures with appropriate comments on what they indicate.

The quality of the information will reflect the following:

(a) The figures are compiled by the borrower who is often lacking in financial training and may be keen to give the bank the information he or she believes it would like to see. The assessment of debenture cover will be strongly influenced by the lender's judgment of the reliability of the person in this respect. The company's position will be presented as favourably as possible by the borrower and it needs to be recognised that in areas such as stock and work in progress, the borrower has a large amount of scope to 'improve' the figures.

(b) The worse the company's position is seen to be, the less reliance should be placed on the reported figures, because as cash becomes tighter, the more quickly will good assets be realised, resulting in those of lesser quality constituting a high proportion of the figures.

The reliability of the information supplied should be reflected in the debenture formula. Stronger formulae would be required from those borrowers whose capacity for providing accurate figures is regarded as suspect. Periodic confirmation of the figures (say quarterly) by the company's auditor can always be requested when there is reason to doubt the company's figures.

Different lenders will have different recording forms for debenture monitoring information. The debenture figures requested from borrowers should include a breakdown of debtors, creditors and stock to be compared with bank borrowing. If information is also sought on capital expenditure and movements in other borrowing, an analysis in the form of a rudimentary Sources and Applications of Funds statement can be produced, so that not only can the debenture formula be monitored, but also trends which can show what is happening to the underlying profits and liquidity performance of the business. Whenever the analysis raises questions which cannot be answered, or reveals a worsening trend, it is vital to act without delay.

If the figures indicate that the agreed debenture formula cannot be maintained, the lender may be asked to agree to a less stringent formula. Agreeing to such a request would be the same as releasing security and it might be preferable from the lender's point of view to accept a temporary breach, rather than agreeing to a permanent relaxation which could be difficult to restore later.

(G) GUARANTEES AND OTHER THIRD PARTY SECURITY

This section will deal with some of the practical aspects of taking guarantees from corporate borrowers.

Whether a company can validly give a guarantee or any other third party charge depends on the following factors.

Capacity of the Company

(a) The first thing to establish is whether the company's Memorandum of Association expressly deals with the giving of guarantees/third party charges.

If there is a specific paragraph in the Memorandum, a distinction still has to be made between the 'main objects' of the company and those provisions in its objects clause which empower the company to enter into transactions in furtherance of its main objects.

A provision is often found at the end of the objects clause, such as 'it is hereby expressly declared that each of the preceding sub-clauses shall be construed independently of and shall be in no way limited by reference to any other sub-clause and that the objects set out in each sub-clause are independent objects of the company'. This provision is intended to convey that each paragraph of the objects clause can be regarded as an independent main object of the company.

It is by no means certain that such a provision will achieve its purpose in practice and it should be treated with extreme caution. There are times when it can be effective. With a finance company, for example, it may be possible to construe the power to give guarantees as one of its main objects. Such a power in the objects clause of a trading company, however, only implies that it can be exercised for the purposes of a company's main objects. In fact this implied restriction may be expressly stated if the guarantee power uses qualifying language such as 'for the purposes of the company's business'.

To summarise, a paragraph in the objects clause might be regarded as a power, and not a main object, if:

(i)   the subject matter of the paragraph by its very nature cannot constitute a main object of the company;
(ii)   the wording of the objects clause shows expressly or implicitly that the paragraph should operate as an ancillary power only.

(b) If the giving of guarantees/third party security is regarded as a power, it can only be exercised for the purpose of, or incidentally to, the main objects of the company.
(c) There might be other limitations incorporated in the power to give guarantees/third party charges. The power might restrict the class of persons in respect of which guarantees can be given. A common provision refers to the giving of guarantees for 'customers and others'. It is generally considered that the term 'and others' is confined to persons in some way connected with the company. It will, therefore, apply to other members of the same group of companies, but not necessarily other third parties. Moreover, if security is to be taken in support of a guarantee, a check will have to be made on the power to give charges. A power to charge by way of security for 'borrowings' cannot be relied on for supporting guarantees.

Whenever a lender is in doubt of the existence or scope of powers to guarantee or to give third party charges, legal guidance should be sought. A suitable form of words which a company can be asked to incorporate in its objects clause by special resolution of its shareholders can then be drawn up.

Authority of the Directors

Having established the company's capacity to give a guarantee, it is then necessary to determine whether the transaction is within the authority of the directors.

They are agents of the company and have an obligation to exercise the company's powers in a proper manner. In order for the guarantee to be valid, the directors must have:

(a) given actual consideration to the position of the company in giving the proposed guarantee;
(b) been satisfied that the transaction was in the interests of the company itself (not some third party), and,

(c) acted in good faith in reaching their decision.

If these conditions can be satisfied, the courts will not intervene. It is for the directors alone to determine whether something is in the interests of the company. However, if a guarantee is given in such circumstances where no reasonable board of directors could have genuinely and in good faith reached such a decision and the lender had express notice of that or the facts were such as to put the lender on enquiry, then the transaction could be challenged.

A prudent lender will always seek express evidence that the company's position has been considered and that the giving of a guarantee is believed to be in the company's best interests, in the form of a Board Resolution. In addition, it may be wise for the lender to separately consider whether it was reasonable for the directors to reach their decision given the surrounding circumstances and not proceed unless the position is clear.

Intra-group Guarantees

Many of the corporate guarantees which a lender takes are to support facilities granted to other limited companies within a group. A subsidiary can give a guarantee to its parent or a fellow subsidiary provided each transaction is in its interests. This might be where there is an inter-company trading relationship between members of a group; or where insolvencies might occur within the group as a result of failure by the group in totality to obtain new or extended facilities. The argument would be that even though the subsidiary itself might not be brought down, such insolvencies would adversely affect the market perception or the available terms of trade for the subsidiary itself.

Provided that it is in its interests, a company can give an unlimited guarantee even where the contingent liability exceeds its assets. However, the greater the dependence on the guarantee and the greater the potential liability in relation to company assets, the more carefully the directors should have thought about the matter in the context of the company's interests.

Parent Company Guarantees

Benefit can be assumed in all cases where a parent company guarantees a subsidiary.

Care needs to be exercised however when assessing the value of such a guarantee. The guarantee is being given by the parent company as a legal entity in itself and it is the strength of the sole balance sheet of the parent which has to be assessed, not the consolidated balance sheet of the group. Many parent companies are merely holding companies whose main assets are the shares of subsidiaries, with the subsidiaries themselves holding the main trading assets of the business. If the subsidiaries get into difficulty or fail, the parent's investment in them, and therefore the assets supporting the guarantee, could be worthless.

In situations where a parent is just a holding company, it would be necessary to have guarantees from asset owning subsidiaries if the borrowing subsidiary does not stand on its own feet. Whilst this will generally be a good rule, it will not be necessary where a large diversified group is involved. The failure of one or more subsidiaries in such a group may not harm the continued profitable trading of other subsidiaries so that the parent would survive such a situation and its guarantee have a continuing value.

(H)   LETTERS OF COMFORT

These are letters provided by a company to indicate support of the liabilities of a subsidiary, but which are less strong than the standard form of guarantee usually required by a bank.

Letters of Comfort can be drawn up by either the lender or the borrower, can come in many forms and give varying degrees of protection to the lender. There are essentially three types of Letter of Comfort:

1   A short form guarantee/indemnity which will confirm that the liabilities of the subsidiary will be met in full by the company giving the Letter.
2   A form of words which can be construed as a contract between the donor company and the lender, probably containing a form of words along the lines that 'we (donor company) will ensure that the company (the subsidiary) has sufficient funds to discharge its liabilities to you as they fall due'.
3   A form of words which may exclude any legal liability and which will be of moral worth only.

Until recently no UK bank had ever taken legal action over a Letter of Comfort obligation. However, in 1987 Kleinwort Benson Limited won an action in the High Court against the Malaysian Mining Corporation Berhad for breach of contract under a Letter of Comfort with a wording similar to that indicated under point 2 above. The case indicated the importance of the need to ensure the donor company of a Letter of Comfort fully appreciates the obligation it is entering into. One of the key issues in the case was the fact that Malaysian had treated the letter as a document of great consequence, as was evidenced by the fact that it was backed by a formal resolution of their Board. (At the time of writing, the decision of the High Court in the case has been reversed by the Court of Appeal, but the circumstances demonstrate the need for very careful and precise wording of such documents.)

Ideally therefore if Letters of Comfort are to be relied on, they should be signed pursuant to a Board Resolution and be renewed at regular intervals so that the position remains clear to all parties.

9 CORPORATE BORROWERS—WHEN THINGS GO WRONG

This chapter will examine what can be done when corporate lending goes wrong, and the steps which need to be taken to minimise the risk and potential loss.

The following aspects will be considered:

(a) General considerations
(b) Warning signs
(c) Immediate action
(d) Whether to lend more
(e) Taking remedial action
(f) Losing unsatisfactory business
(g) Cross firing
(h) Using investigating accountants

(A) GENERAL CONSIDERATIONS

Lending is a risky business, and it is inevitable that on occasions things will go wrong, so that with hindsight it appears that a bad decision has been taken. No criticism should be levelled at a lender who has made a reasonable decision based on all the known facts at the time. What does warrant criticism is a lending going wrong as a result of a failure to recognise obvious warning signs and to take remedial action when it becomes apparent that plans have gone awry.

Nobody likes to see themselves proved wrong, and there will always be a temptation to indulge in wishful thinking that any problem is only temporary and the borrower will get things right in the end. Objectivity is needed at a time when it is hard to be objective. The original lending decision may well have been soundly based but a new, and adverse, factor will have been brought into the lending equation and a new appraisal of the position will be necessary. The mistake needs to be admitted at an early stage, and if the lender then finds difficulty in being objective on the way forward, the situation should be discussed with senior colleagues before any further commitment is made.

(B) WARNING SIGNS

As has been stated earlier in this book, the monitoring of accounts is the boring part of lending. It is easy in practice to down grade its importance when there are lots of other things to do. This is a mistake; research has shown that the bad debt performance of the major banks would have been much better if earlier action had been taken when danger signs became apparent. So, it is necessary always to:

(a) compare actuals against budgets/cash flow forecasts;
(b) make an adequate assessment of debenture figures when supplied;
(c) investigate the reasons for excesses when they appear on the bank account.

In Chapter 7, the main tools available to a bank lender for monitoring borrowing situations were set out in detail. They were:

(a) internal records;
(b) visits and interviews;
(c) audited accounts;
(d) management accounts.

The following is a list of the various danger signs which may become apparent from monitoring in these individual areas. Taken individually, one sign may not cause undue concern, but careful investigation will be necessary where a number of them appear together:

Internal Records

1	Unauthorised excess	10	Special collections in
2	Excess or extra facility sanctioned	11	Special collections out
		12	Status enquiries in
3	Account turnover increasing	13	Status enquiries out
4	Account turnover decreasing	14	County court judgment
5	Hardcore	15	Standing orders—outside borrowing?
6	Unpaid cheques in		
7	Unpaid cheques out	16	Stopped cheques in
8	Round amount cheques	17	Stopped cheques out
9	Uncleareds — cross firing?	18	Cash withdrawals
	— excess coming?	19	Rumours

Visit/Interview

1	Elusive directors	12	Two businesses in one set of premises
2	No long term aims		
3	Failure to meet orders	13	Dead stock
4	Reliance on one customer	14	Creditor pressure (usual cause of excess)
5	Reliance on one supplier		
6	Buying bargains—on the cheap?	15	Management changes
		16	Management old—no succession
7	Diversification		
8	Delays in cash coming in	17	Management team unbalanced
9	Request for release of security (especially guarantees)	18	Management unable to react to changed circumstances
10	Changes in terms of trade	19	Changes in attitude (since last meeting)
11	Idle assets (effect on Return on Capital Employed)		

Audited Accounts

1	Other borrowing	9	Qualified
2	Gearing high	10	Other bankers
3	Surplus small	11	Unusually high audit fee
4	Losses	12	Revalued assets
5	Late	13	Figures strange when compared to management accounts (or debenture figures)
6	Draft		
7	Two sets!		
8	Change of auditor		

Management Accounts

1	Late	7	Targets not met
2	Sketchy	8	No assumptions with forecast
3	Non-existent	9	Losses
4	Debenture formula breached	10	Margin of safety small, reducing
5	Debenture figures strange (when compared to audited accounts or previous figures)	11	Loss of customers
		12	Customers not spread
6	Increase in preferential creditors	13	Pricing by guesswork

When a lender becomes concerned about an account a more detailed monitoring procedure, at least monthly, needs to be instituted. The monitoring will need to concentrate on the following areas:

1   Has the overdraft limit been exceeded in the last three months? This could be due to an unexpected increase in sales—have

working capital requirements been assessed? Or caused by a decrease in sales—have they dropped below the business's break-even point causing losses?

2   Did the borrower not appreciate that an excess was about to occur? This suggests weak or poor cash planning and monitoring by the borrower, or may be an indication that he or she is reluctant to discuss a problem with the lender.

3   Is the average balance on the account over, say, the last six months showing an increasing borrowing trend? Is a hardcore developing?

4   Does turnover through the bank account show a rapid increase or decrease over recent months? This may be an early warning sign of significant increases or decreases in sales. Does the borrower also have a bank account elsewhere?

5   Has there been any recent indication that directors would like to see their personal guarantees and/or personal security released? This would be the logical thing for them to do if they have foreseen real problems.

6   Has the receipt of promised funds been delayed? This could indicate either problems in meeting sales orders or the borrower having customers who may have difficulty in paying.

7   Has it been necessary to return cheques? The borrower's suppliers may restrict trade credit if this is the case, with a consequent knock-on effect greatly increasing a business's working capital needs.

8   Has the number of returned cheques inwards been increasing? This may suggest that the borrower is seeking a poorer quality of business in an attempt to hold up sales.

9   Are cheques being issued in round amounts? This may suggest that 'holding' payments may be being made to appease pressing creditors. It might be evidence of cross firing.

10   Is the promised monitoring information not produced on time? This could suggest inadequate systems, or the borrower not wishing to report a deteriorating situation.

11   Has the company been attempting to borrow elsewhere? There may be a good reason, but why was the lender not approached first, or has the borrowing already been refused?

12   Have apparently key personnel left the business recently? This could be evidence of either conflict amongst the management team or individuals seeking to get out before 'the ship sinks'.

13   Is the company seeking to expand by acquisition? Whilst this may be entirely acceptable, a very capable management team is needed to adequately research and integrate new businesses. There is always the danger of 'buying a pup' and even the biggest companies sometimes get this wrong. For small companies it can be disastrous.

14   Is the debenture formula being met? A reduction in current asset cover may suggest losses, capital expenditure which cannot be afforded or pressing creditors.
15   Do management accounts show a major divergence from budget? Things cannot be expected to go totally to plan, but significant variances must be explained.
16   Are profit margins holding up? Are sales having to be 'bought'? This will be particularly dangerous if a company has a high fixed cost base as the break-even point will have been lowered.
17   Has there been a build up in monies owed to preferential creditors? This can seem to be an easier option to the borrower than not paying trade creditors on whose continued willingness to supply the business will depend. All creditors need to be met on time and the Inland Revenue will often be prepared to act with considerable vigour once they identify a problem.
18   Is there any evidence that increased credit is being taken, or abnormal discounts being given to debtors to make them pay early? This might simply be good cash management practice, but could equally show the business is under real cash pressure.

An adverse answer to any one of the above questions may not be significant, but when a number of the answers suggest problems then early action must be taken.

(C) IMMEDIATE ACTION

It is vital that once potential problems have been identified, speedy and positive action is taken along the following lines:

(a) Investigate the new situation and collect as much information as possible.
(b) Assess the situation. Is more information required?
(c) Is the security position satisfactory? Check to ensure that charges are effective. Is the security margin adequate and/or is additional security available?
(d) Discuss the position in detail with the borrower.
(e) Having assessed the position, decide on a clear objective on the way forward. If full repayment is impossible without incurring greater risk, accept the best return which *is* possible.
(f)   Give the borrower clear but realistic targets in respect of time and amounts.
(g) Control the position firmly and carry any intended actions through. Empty threats will not give the right message to the borrower.

(D) WHETHER TO LEND MORE

Most experienced lenders will recognise situations where they have lent more to a borrower to keep a business going and with the benefit of hindsight have 'thrown good money after bad'. It is often far better to accept a limited loss on a borrowing rather than lending more to a business which is in difficulties in the hope things will improve. In many cases all that will happen is that the lender will be involved in an even greater loss.

Lenders will always want to help businesses which are expanding, and an unexpected request for an increased borrowing may be needed to cover the problems of success with the extra requirement for more working capital or capital expenditure that these can bring. The borrower's original plan should have had sufficient margin for error built into its assumptions to cover foreseeable contingencies, and any request for increased borrowing is likely to be unwelcome to the lender. Under what circumstances should the lender be prepared to increase the borrowing, and when should such a request be refused? A full re-appraisal of the business must be carried out in the light of the new circumstances. The following factors should be taken into account:

(a) Management—there has by definition been a failure on the part of management. Either sufficient margin for contingencies was not built into the original plan or there has been a failure of performance. Management may have learned by its mistakes, but has it learned enough?

The question of the management's integrity must also be considered. Did they realise that there was a significant risk of their plan going awry, but not make this clear to the lender? Have they been scrupulously honest? Did they, for example, use the borrowing wholly for the purpose for which it was originally granted?

If the management of a business cannot be trusted, it would be foolish to lend more.

(b) Underlying assumptions—there will have been certain key assumptions which formed the basis of budget forecasts. There will now be actual information on performance to test how these have worked out in practice.

If one or more major assumptions has been found to be incorrect, can even a revised plan be made to work? Has a new plan been produced incorporating more realistic assumptions?

(c) Trends—the borrower must produce sufficiently detailed information on performance to date to enable the lender to judge the direction in which the key elements of the business are moving.

If expected growth in the business is not being seen, then new forecasts must be produced to reflect this. A lender needs to be particularly sceptical if recent performance has been flat, but updated projections assume considerable growth.

(d) Security margin—the previous chapter looked at what an adequate security margin would be for a corporate lending. If the margin was only just adequate when the original lending was made it would be illogical for the lender to allow it to be reduced just when the risk in the lending has increased because the borrower has failed to perform.

A lender might be willing to lend more if there was originally a wide security margin or additional security is available. But, caution is necessary and the lending should not be increased simply to obtain some further perhaps poor quality security. For example, taking a second charge over a small equity in a matrimonial home may not in practice increase the chances of recovery, particularly if the lending is being increased.

(e) Risk—lending more on the back of a poor performance, particularly against reduced net assets or a fixed level of security, will inevitably involve the lender in undertaking a higher risk. There is a need to project an assessment of the borrower's potential position in, say, six months' time if performance continues to be poor. On a worst case analysis, what would the lender's write-off be? This can then be compared with the lender's probable loss now if no more is lent.

The question that then needs to be answered is: is the extra risk really worth it? The lender will not be helping the customer if the borrowing is increased against a poor chance of projections being achieved. It can often be best for both borrower and lender to cut their losses at an early stage.

(E) TAKING REMEDIAL ACTION

When a company is in difficulties, action will generally need to be taken to improve profitability. However, businesses do not go into liquidation through a lack of profits, they do so because they run out of cash. In the short term therefore the problem company will need to make the best use of the limited cash resources which are available. In order to do this, it will have to ensure that:

(a) Profit margins are set at a level to both generate adequate demand and cash flow.
(b) All assets in the business are fully utilised.

All the areas of the business which tie up cash need to be examined in detail to see if improvements can be made. The lender needs to question the company closely as to what is being done under the following headings:

Stock
— concentrate on the few items which will have the biggest impact in cash terms
— tighten physical security if stock is 'attractive'
— reduce overall levels if production still viable
— reduce re-order quantities
— dispose of slow moving/obsolete stock
— consider alternative suppliers re i) price
                                                 ii) credit given
— shorter production runs (may affect profitability)

Debtors
— tighten initial vetting
— review invoicing system
— review credit terms
— ensure terms *met* (particularly if discounts for early payment are given)
— obtain progress payments (*care:* this may reduce profitability)
— consider factoring for i) improved efficiency
                                      ii) reduced fixed costs
                                      iii) speedier receipt
                                      iv) possible use of finance facility
— consider invoice discounting if appropriate.

Creditors
— do not take discounts *if cash short* (otherwise can be *very profitable*)
— find alternatives (see Stock)
— re-negotiate term loans (if possible)

Assets
— dispose of surplus assets
— consider sale and leaseback
— lease rather than buy

Products
— which are 'cash hungry'?
— which have the better 'turn' (even if longer-term profitability may suffer)?
— where is the product on its 'cycle' life?

— if products dropped—will company then be losing
'contribution' to fixed costs which will continue anyway?
— which products does the company 'like' to produce and which
should it produce?
— concentrate on the few items which will have the biggest impact
on profits/cashflow

Labour
— consider reduction in staffing if possible
— consider sub-contract labour (can save large sums of working
capital otherwise tied up in stocks, etc)
— consider union problems if above undertaken

Capital Expenditure
— consider new projects very carefully
— review appraisal technique
— review existing projects in pipeline—are they continuing because
a great deal has been spent already or because they will really
be viable and cash producing in the near future? It is frequently
better to cut one's losses now and make more money later on a
less cash-hungry venture
— review plans for research
— review expensive advertising campaigns

Management
— can they be trusted to take 'hard' decisions?
— is a change needed?
— consider reducing numbers
— if a family company—who has the power to replace?
— do they need outside advice? Would investigating accountants
help?

(F)   LOSING UNSATISFACTORY BUSINESS

When a problem business has been identified and it becomes clear
that matters are not going to improve, the logical step is to get rid
of it. Some major banks, for example, set their branch managers
a target of losing their five or six worst accounts to another bank
every year. Lenders are often reluctant to push away marginal business
as, whilst the risk is high, so are the rewards. There will often be
a temptation to try to control the risk and to extract that bit more
profit from the situation. The danger is that the lender hangs on
just too long and the opportunity to get rid of a future loss passes
by.

It will almost always be a mistake to continue with a business until it is formally wound up if it was possible to get rid of it earlier. The previous chapter gave an indication of the sort of discount factors which have to be applied to book assets in a break up situation. It would be foolish of the lender to unnecessarily take on the risk of reducing going concern asset values by the sort of discounts involved. Assumed asset values very often turn out to be optimistic in a winding up and realisations are rarely as good as anticipated at the outset.

Precisely when should unsatisfactory business be pushed away? The somewhat paradoxical answer is—whilst it still seems potentially viable. Getting rid of problem business works on the 'bigger fool' theory. The lender has to hope that there will be someone who will still take the business even though it has problems. In Chapter 1, caution was advised before taking over a lending from another bank, so it must be expected that any problem business will be looked at with a degree of scepticism. It must therefore be offered to other lenders at a stage when a plausible case can be made for providing a lending. It follows that the business must be lost at a stage when any lender (and that includes the current lender) would still be willing to give the borrower the benefit of the doubt.

The current lender will have the advantage of having seen the business operate at close quarters and will therefore have a detailed knowledge of the borrower's track record. The new lender will lack this knowledge, particularly in areas where subjective assessments have to be made, such as the borrower's management abilities or market prospects. Thus when it appears that one of these underlying fundamental elements of a business is going wrong, but this fact has not yet become apparent to any significant extent in the records of the business's performance, then the chance of finding a 'bigger fool' may be good.

There is always a good profit to be made from high risk business provided it does not result in bad debts. Lenders have to be very skilled—and very careful—when dealing with such companies. By definition, some (probably over half) marginal lendings will go wrong. It follows therefore that a lender undertaking marginal business must be particularly attuned to the need to lose it to another lender when warning signs appear.

(G)   CROSS FIRING

Cross firing is the creation of an apparent credit balance on an account or series of accounts by taking advantage of the delays inherent in the United Kingdom cheque clearing system.

An example as to how this can be done using accounts at three different branches is set out below:

	Debits	Credits	Balance
Branch 'X'			
Jan 1 Cheque per 'Z'		2,000	CR 2,000
2 Cheque per 'Y'		8,000	10,000
3 Cheque to 'Y'	2,000		8,000
4 Cheque per 'Z'		16,000	
4 Cheque to 'Z'	8,000		16,000
Branch 'Y'			
Jan 1 Cheque per 'X'		2,000	2,000
2 Cheque per 'Z'		8,000	10,000
3 Cheque to 'Z'	2,000		8,000
4 Cheque per 'X'		16,000	
4 Cheque to 'X'	8,000		16,000
Branch 'Z'			
Jan 1 Cheque per 'Y'		2,000	2,000
2 Cheque per 'X'		8,000	10,000
3 Cheque to 'X'	2,000		8,000
4 Cheque per 'Y'		16,000	
4 Cheque to 'Y'	8,000		16,000

Once the perpetrator uses the artificial credit established to make a payment outside the ring of accounts involved and the bank has allowed it to happen, nothing can prevent a corresponding loss being incurred by one of the parties. At its worst, cross firing is a criminal attempt to defraud a bank, but it could also be a despairing means for a business with cash problems to stay within its overdraft limit. However, once started, cross firing can expand very rapidly.

Losses to the banks from major cross firing frauds have been known to run into millions of pounds. Although in its simplest form cross firing will only involve two accounts, complex transactions can involve many individuals passing cheques in a ring, and there may be great difficulty in relating them.

Detecting Cross Firing

There is a need to be alert to the possibility of cross firing occurring and to examine suspicious transactions. The following points represent a guide to the detection of cross firing:

(a) Be aware of the possibility of cross firing when monitoring accounts generally.

(b) Does the account show a large turnover whilst only small balances are maintained without there being an adequate explanation? Sudden and unexplained increases in turnover should be particularly suspect.

(c) Do the credit balances on an account represent cleared funds? It is in the payment of cheques against uncleared effects when the risk of loss occurs.

(d) Are cheques paid in payable to 'cash' or parties connected to the drawers?

(e) Are cheques for round sums paid in? Surprisingly this is often the case with cross firing, but the clever operator will seek to disguise the transactions.

(f) The bank crossings on customers paid cheques may help in linking up connections with districts and parties and with the drawee banks of cheques paid in.

(g) It is with the little known or customer in difficulties where the highest risk will occur.

Cross firing is relatively rare, and there are many transactions between accounts or inter-company transactions which are quite genuine. It is where transactions involve the payment against uncleared effects that caution is required.

(H) USING INVESTIGATING ACCOUNTANTS

There will often come a point when a lending is not going well when the lender is no longer prepared to simply rely on the borrower's assessment of a business's future prospects, and decides that an independent expert investigation of the position is required. This will usually be carried out by an investigating accountant. The accountant will need to come from a firm experienced in insolvency work. The size of the firm to be used will depend on the likely complexity of the investigation which is to be carried out.

Bank charge forms do not incorporate any power to insist upon an investigation and, in any case, the borrower's co-operation will be needed. The borrower needs to be persuaded that the investigation is necessary, but will often be reluctant both because of the likely cost, which the borrower will have to pay, and the implication that the investigation is merely the prelude to a winding up.

It needs to be stressed to the borrower that an investigation is not necessarily a preliminary step automatically followed by winding up, but may point the way to improvements which can save the company. The important thing is for any investigation to be undertaken well in advance of a business entering its terminal stages.

Timing

The general view of insolvency practitioners is that lenders are too slow in seeking independent opinions on marginal businesses.

It is obviously easier to persuade a borrower to ask for an investigation when he has no realistic alternative, than at an earlier point when the argument will be put forward that an investigation is not necessary. The fact that the investigation is required will show the business's management that the lender has little confidence in the information they are producing, and the cost will not be welcome at a time when cash resources and profitability are under strain.

If the borrower is to be convinced of a need for an investigation at an early enough stage, the lender will have to make the best use of his bargaining position. This will generally mean not increasing the lending facilities available until an independent assessment is made.

One important point which needs to be considered before an investigation is undertaken is that the existence of an independent report will crystallise the situation. If it is hoped to lose the account to another bank, this will no longer be a realistic possibility once an adverse investigating accountant's report exists. It may also be difficult at that stage to take additional security in, say, the form of increased directors' guarantees. These things must be done before an investigation takes place.

Terms of Reference

An investigating accountant's brief must be tailored to the individual circumstances, but the lender will generally request a report covering the following areas:

1 (a) brief introduction;
   (b) conclusions, and recommendations as to the action that should be taken by the company and/or the lender.
2 Brief description of business including:
   (a) activities;
   (b) location(s);
   (c) management/key employees (including total number of employees and locations).
3 Comments on:
   (a) The financial position of the company at a given date with comments on the following:

     (i)   The facilities, outstandings and security held by all lenders to the company, whether on or off balance sheet and including contingent liabilities.

     (ii) Creditor spread and age analysis.

     (iii) Debtors and age analysis.

     (iv) Bad debt record.

     (v)   Stock valuation and breakdown.

     (vi) Adequacy of existing stock and debtor provisions and need for new provisions.

     (vii) Any relevant matters regarding taxation.

     (viii) Profit performance for the current year to date.

  (b) The last two full years' results, either audited or draft.

4   Comments on or preparation of:

  (a) Cash flow forecast for the company on a monthly (weekly if felt appropriate) basis, to cover the next three month period.

  (b) Suggested means of dealing with the immediate liquidity problem.

5   Preparation or review of:

  (a) The monthly projected profit and loss accounts and cash flow forecasts for the company.

     (i)   To the end of the current financial year, and

     (ii) For such part of the next financial year as is necessary to cover a 12-month period from the date of the report.

  (b) The projected balance sheet for the current year and quarterly periods before then (if any) and as at the quarterly period(s) during the next financial year, to cover projections for at least 12 months forward.

Comment specifically on the underlying assumptions used in (a) and (b) and on any sensitivity analysis which may be considered necessary and can be carried out.

6   Comments on:

  (a) the costing systems used;

  (b) the method of taking profit on contracts;

  (c) any contracts thought to be unprofitable.

7   Comments on:

  (a) the prospects of the company;

  (b) the contribution which individual activities make to profits or losses;

  (c) any further provisions required, particularly against stocks and on any possible claims for retention of title;

  (d) adequacy of the company's financing arrangements.

8   Observations on:

  (a) management and financial controls;

  (b) information systems;

(c) the suitability of the present management and corporate structure of the business(es);

(d) reorganisation and cost saving possibilities.

9   The extent of the security cover available to the lender:

(a) on a going concern basis;

(b) on a break-up basis.

For facilities to the company:

(a) now;

(b) quarterly over the next 12-month period.

10 Any other matters which may appear to be relevant to the company's viability and the position of their lenders, together with a view of the action needed to:

(a) achieve rationalisation to stop losses;

(b) improve profitability;

(c) improve cash flow;

(d) reduce borrowings so as to ensure the company's survival in the short and long term.

Because an investigation is always technically requested by the borrower rather than the lender, the accountant's brief will be to produce a report for the borrower. It will not therefore cover one major area on which the lender will always want an independent opinion—the quality of the borrower's management. However investigating accountants will expect to report informally to lenders on this area, and indeed many businesses have been saved through investigating accountants finding replacement management for those who have proved to be incompetent.

PART D

SPECIAL KINDS OF LENDING

10 ADVANCES TO BUILDERS

The term 'builder' covers a wide area of activities from major civil engineering work, such as road building contracts and drainage schemes, through hospitals, schools, government housing schemes, factories, and private housing down to small extensions.

As well as lending money, the bank could be asked to provide guarantees/bonds, which must be regarded as real liabilities since, if called, the amount of the guarantee/bond might have to be advanced in addition to other facilities.

CONTRACT BUILDING

Appraisal of the Proposition

Although the subject matter here is builders, the following comments will apply equally to many other types of contracting business. The usual approach will be for the lender to always closely investigate the details of specific contracts, unless of course the customer is very experienced and successful in the contracting business and is financially sound. Reliance can simply be placed on the level of security cover available, but difficulties can arise as a result of inadequate capital resources or by inexperience in tendering for contracts. Unless the borrower can satisfy the lender in these respects, a full examination of the contract should be carried out.

The usual lending criteria will apply, but the following additional points will have to be considered:

(a) Is the customer experienced in the industry and in the type of work proposed?
(b) Can reliance be placed on the borrower's costings?
(c) Does the borrower have adequate financial resources?
(d) The details of the contract.
(e) The factors influencing the amount required.

The Contract

It is vital that the borrower has the capacity to complete the contract.

For example, a contract for £200,000 for completion in 12 months will require approximately £4,000 of work per week.

In checking the contract, the lender needs to be on the look out for clauses covering the following:

— Variations—although the contract price will be open to adjustment in respect of variations, these might mean that additional finance is required. This will be particularly true if the variations are so large as to alter materially the scope of the contract or if payments are to be made on a different time basis to other payments.
— Fluctuations in cost—particularly necessary in longer term contracts where the builder would be vulnerable to increases in materials' costs and wages during the period of the contract.
— Penalties—these can be extremely onerous, and the borrower must have the capability and self-discipline to plan a strict schedule and see that it is maintained.
— Extension of time—to permit extensions under specified circumstances such as Force Majeure, extremely bad weather, strikes, civil commotions, variations, etc.
— Interim payments—the intervals (usually monthly) at which the work will be inspected by the architect and certificates issued in respect of the work completed. Also set out will be the time lag between certification and payment, which is often stated as 14 days. However it would be unwise for both the builder and the lender to rely on prompt payment of certificates, as delays are often experienced.
— Retention fund—usually either 5% or 10% of contract price. This will build up from monies withheld from interim payments, although half of the fund might be released as soon as the work is completed.
— Period of final measurement—often six months after completion of the work. During this period, the architect or quantity surveyor is required to thoroughly inspect the work, verify previous measurements and amounts certified for payment and, in particular, check and agree figures for any extra work which may be needed to be carried out (variations). Payment for these variations is often deferred to the end of the Period of Final Measurement.
— Defects liability period—often six months, to allow latent defects to show through. These must be rectified at the builder's expense, and the final certificate will not be issued until the architect is satisfied that this has been done. The builder will then receive the remainder of the Retention Fund.

— Nominated sub-contractors and suppliers—these have the right to go to the employer if payment is not received from the builder when due. In such circumstances the contract will authorise the employer to make payment and deduct monies paid from amounts due to the builder. Where significant sums are involved, it is prudent to check that such suppliers and sub-contractors are being paid regularly.

— Other matters—some government and local authority contracts include provisions such as: 'all constructional plant, temporary works and material owned by the contractor or by any company in which the contractor has a controlling interest shall, when brought on the site (or in the case of hire purchase plant on its becoming the property of the contractor), immediately be deemed to become the property of the employer.' The employer is defined as the person or organisation employing the contractor so such a clause could be onerous and affect a lender's security.

Amount

The lender must be certain that the amount requested will, when added to the borrower's own capital input, be sufficient for the contract to be completed. Otherwise, the lender will have no alternative but to lend more than is desirable, and/or be faced with a possible bad debt. The following section gives a basis for calculating the required amount and what would be a reasonable level of capital input from the builder:

(a) What is the minimum amount required to enable the contract to be concluded successfully?

The calculation which follows assumes that the work can be spread evenly over the term of the contract. This will rarely, if ever, be possible in practice. A number of things can cause delays (e.g. bad weather, strikes, late delivery of materials, etc.), consequently the sight of sizeable fluctuations in the work done month by month is a familiar characteristic of most contracts. Variations increasing the scope of the work would also result in an increase in the total finance requirement.

In practice, a substantial reserve should be provided for contingencies and the lender will be looking for the builder to have formalised the calculations in a budget and cash flow forecast.

Calculation of minimum finance required to complete a building contract

Contract price	—	£118,000	
Time allowed for work	—	9 months	
Interim Certificates	—	monthly (NB: *In these calculations 30 days are allowed as delays are commonly experienced*)	
Period for honouring Interim Certificates	—	14 days	
Retentions to be at rate of	—	10%	
Limit of Retention Fund	—	£5,900 (5% of total contact)	
Calculation	—	Contract price	£118,000
		Deduct estimated profit	£ 23,600
		Estimated cost to builder	£ 94,400

As work is to take 9 months—estimated average monthly cost $\left(\dfrac{£94,400}{9}\right)$ = £ 10,500

It is necessary to distinguish between cost of labour and cost of materials and for the purpose of this example it is assumed that costs are in the proportion of two thirds (labour) and one third (materials).

Hence, monthly average costs:

Labour	£ 7,000
Materials	£ 3,500
Total	£10,500

The builder will work a month before the first certificate is issued and thereafter may have to wait a further month before payment is made, i.e., it will be approximately two months from commencing work before his first payment is received.

During this time he will have to provide:

2 months' wages @ £7,000		£14,000
2 months' materials @ £3,500	£7,000	
(less 1 month's credit from merchant)	£3,500	£ 3,500
Total finance required to reach stage of first payment		£17,500

At this stage the builder will receive payment for the amount of work certified (for the first month)—less 10% retention. Ignoring the profit element, therefore, he will require additional finance in subsequent months to cover the 'shortfall' due to retentions. This position will continue until the full amount of retention fund is held by the employer. (Thereafter payments will be for the full amount certified so that receipts should balance outgoings—indeed, they should exceed outgoings if the work is yielding a profit).

The total cash resources required can therefore be estimated at:

Finance to reach first payment (as above)	£17,500
Limit of Retention Fund	£ 5,900
	£23,400 (minimum)

(b) How much of the finance should be provided from the builders' own resources? It is implied that the difference between this and the minimum required finance will be provided by the lender.

It is a well tested principle that before approaching a lender for assistance, the builder should always have acquired the plant and be in a position to carry out the contract at least to the point where his second payment from the employer is certified and due.

Calculation of finance which the lender would expect the builder to provide from his own resources

Time	Particulars	Paid by builder
		£
Start	Work commences	
End of first month	First certificate issued	
	Wages paid during month (materials on credit from merchant)	7,000
End of second month	second certificate issued	
	First certificate paid	
	Less: retention	
	Wages paid during month	7,000
	Payment for first month's materials	3,500
	(Second month's materials on credit)	
		17,500

Deduct payment for first certificate
(⅑th contract price less 10% retention)

i.e. $\dfrac{118,000}{9}$ (13,100 – £1,300)   11,800
                                                                 5,700

End of third
month   third certificate issued
                         Payment for second
                         certificate now due
                         Wages paid during month   7,000
Amount outstanding before second payment
certified and due   £12,700

NB: In terms of the contract the second payment was due 14
     days after the end of second month. By the end of the third
     month payment for the second month's materials becomes
     due. Third month's materials on credit.

From the figures in the specimen calculations, i.e. finance required
£23,400 (say, £23,500), amount to be provided by builder £12,700
(say, £12,500) we calculate that he would require the assistance
of the bank to the extent of £11,000.

Provided there is satisfactory evidence that the builder will
have the £12,500 available, a limit of £11,000 might be considered
and it would be reasonable to expect to see the contract completed
fairly comfortably within this figure.

It is important that lenders do not view the above calculations
as a simple 'rule of thumb', because the proportion of the total
cost which the builder should provide, and the amount of cash
required, will vary considerably for different contracts.

Monitoring and Control of Contract Advances

The pro-forma set out on the next page is a useful aid when a builder
has several contracts in operation at the same time. It will be necessary
for the builder to complete one of these forms at monthly intervals
and, when comparisons are made from month to month, it is possible
to see:

(a) Whether work is being maintained, i.e. is the total work done
     to date increasing by the average monthly amount required to
     complete the various contracts on time?
(b) Whether work is being certified regularly, i.e. the total amount
     certified should equate with the previous month's figure for 'work

CONTROL OF CONTRACT ADVANCES

SPECIMEN MONTHLY RETURN OF CONTRACT POSITIONS ETC.

(Note that this specimen has been drawn up as a composite form to include most, if not all, of the information likely to be needed in various cases. In practice a simpler ruling suited to the needs of each particular case is likely to be used. The Balance Sheet (Section e.) is often dispensed with).

Contract Particulars	Amount of Contract £	Work Done to Date £	Amount Certified £	Payments received £	Cert. but not Paid nor Retained £	W IN P Not Certified £	Retentions £	Work Outstanding £	Date for Completion	Bond: Amount- Expiry date £
a. *Completed Contracts*										
X.U.D.C.	72,000	72,000	72,000	68,400	—	—	3,600	—	—	7,200 (1/1/88)
b. *Contracts in hand*										
X.U.D.C.	108,000	36,000	24,000	10,800	12,000	12,000	1,200	72,000	1st Oct	10,800 (1/4/88)
Y. Boro' C.C.	80,000	48,000	44,000	34,200	6,000	4,000	3,800	32,000	1st Jan	8,000 (1/7/88)
c. *Contracts not started*										
X.U.D.C.	36,000	—	—	—	—	—	—	—	—	—
	156,000	140,000	113,400	18,000	16,000	8,600	104,000		26,000	
d. *Miscellaneous work*		2,000					500	1,500		

e. Summary of current position —

	£
Trade creditors	10,600
Other creditors	1,900
Bank	12,300
Outstanding cheques	1,800
	26,600
Liquid surplus	13,900
	40,500

	£
Retentions	8,600
Contract debtors	18,000
Other debtors	500
Work in progress	17,500
Stock	4,500
	40,500

N.B. Materials on sites when contract work is being done will usually be included in the figures in columns 3 & 4 above. The 'stock' figure in the balance sheet is therefore usually only stock in builder's own yard.

done to date'. If not certified regularly what is the reason—substandard work, bad relations with the employer's officials, or an inflated figure of 'work done' in the earlier return?
(c) Whether previous payments due have been received.
(d) Whether the builder's financial position is sound or whether resources are stretched. If contracts are profitable, it should reflect in an increase as work proceeds, in the liquid surplus shown in the summary.
(e) Whether regular and prompt payment is being made to creditors.

A note should be made that when audited accounts are available, they should be compared with the figures on the relevant monthly statement.

Building Agreements and Contracts as Security

Building Agreements
These can vary in format, but normally they initially grant the builder only a licence to develop the estate owner's land, usually at the builder's expense. When part or all of the building operations have been satisfactorily completed, the estate owner may:

(a) Grant to the builder on pre-arranged terms a lease or other legal interest in the land.
(b) Grant to an eventual purchaser, a lease or conveyance, with or without the builder joining in the Deed. The builder's rights in the latter case will be restricted to receiving, in certain circumstances, part of the consideration paid to the estate owner; normally no actual interest in the land will be acquired by the builder so that a lender would not be able to look to the property as security.

Restrictive provisions are seen in many building agreements (particularly those in category (b) above), such as limitations on the type of property and the manner of construction, the price to be charged and the choice of eventual buyers, who might have to be on a local authority housing list.

    Payment for the grant of such an agreement could incorporate an initial premium, a percentage or fixed sum out of the proceeds of each property, or a combination of them all. The estate owner will, in some cases, take a proportion of the eventual profit in accordance with the formula incorporated in the agreement. Details of such arrangements may be set out in ancillary documents rather than the actual agreement itself. There might be provision that, in order to prevent the loss of further rights, the builder has to purchase any unsold properties.

It would be prudent for a lender to seek legal advice before entering into binding commitments to advance monies against the security of the type of agreement detailed in category (b).

It is vital to remember that security in the form of any type of building agreement cannot be equated with a charge over the actual land. The majority of such agreements provide for the loss of all interests in the property should the builder fail to comply with the precise terms of the agreement. Such interest can be taken over by the estate owner, without necessarily involving payment of any compensation to either the builder or lender, even if the latter had a mortgage over the builder's interest in the agreement.

Building Contracts

There is a significant difference between building agreements and building contracts. The latter are contracts which provide for a builder to construct buildings on the estate owner's land, where ownership of the land is retained by the estate owner. The builder merely receives payment for work done.

Security can be taken in the form of a charge over the future debt. Sometimes, a building agreement will incorporate a building contract, providing for the receipt of monies by the builder from the estate owner. It is perfectly feasible for this part of the agreement to be charged, irrespective of whether the underlying agreement itself is being charged.

Charges over building contracts do not in practice tend to have a great deal of value. This is because, if the builder fails and does not complete the contract—the circumstances in which the lender will be relying on the security—the employer will have a counter claim for breach of contract and cannot be expected to pay for previous work done.

SPECULATIVE BUILDING

Building which is carried out without definite sales having been arranged in advance is normally defined as speculative building.

All manufacturers of goods rely on ability and judgment to create a product which hopefully the public will buy. A speculative housebuilder is no different. What is different is the considerable cost incurred in building one unit, which increases the risk to the builder, and consequently to the lender.

This section on the speculative development of land will concentrate on a builder developing a housing estate, although the same principles, slightly modified, will apply equally to office and flat developments, etc.

Very often speculative development of houses, offices, shops, flats, etc. is not done by the actual builder, but by some sort of property developer, who will have entered into a contract with a builder to carry out the construction. As regards the financing of the development however, the principles are the same. To avoid any confusion, the borrower will be referred to throughout as the 'developer'.

Financing the Building of Housing Estate

General Examination of Proposed Development

(a) Is the size and nature of the development within the developer's building capacity and experience?
(b) Has confirmation of full planning permission been seen?
(c) The site details must be investigated—in particular any potential problems in respect of drainage, clearance or levelling.
(d) Market feasibility, with particular reference to:

    (i)   Are existing houses in the area selling without difficulty being experienced?
    (ii) Will there be a ready market for the proposed houses?
    (iii) Are the proposed houses of a type and size suitable for the locality?
    (iv) In a mixed development, will all the houses be equally marketable?
    (v) Is the local unemployment level above or below the national average?
    (vi) Are any new businesses coming into the area, which would create a new demand for housing?
    (vii) What level of wages are earned on average?

(e) Is the development conveniently sited for shops, schools, public transport, amenities.
(f) Is a car necessary for access to work or schools—will local traffic conditions discourage would be purchasers?
(g) Will the proposals be affected by local land and/or tax legislation?

How Much Will It Cost?

Detailed figures will be required from the developer showing:

(a) Cost of land (if relevant). Is the price or valuation realistic, based on local knowledge of the area?
(b) Cost of preparing land for development and of providing roads, drainage, sewers, etc. Special care is required as this cost element is often underestimated and usually has to be incurred at the outset.
(c) Building cost of individual houses, including adequate allowance for cost escalation.
(d) Legal and selling expenses.
(e) Overheads including directors' remuneration, administration and finance costs.

It is usually more efficient to build a number of adjoining houses at the same time, especially as this will maximise the utilisation of particular types of skilled labour, etc.

However the ability to do this will depend on the total finance available and on the extent of the lender's willingness to accept uncompleted houses as security in the early stages. Agreement has to be reached between the developer and lender on the number of houses to be built at any one time—the 'phasing' of the development—this has to be reflected in the projections and the lending plan.

Price

(a) Selling prices of the houses have to be established, ideally by reference to an independent estate agent with local knowledge.
(b) Will the prices result in a satisfactory profit margin after allowance for interest and contingencies?

How Much Should the Developer Contribute?

There will be times when it is considered prudent to advance not more than half of the total cost of the overall project, whilst on other occasions it may be considered safe to lend more, depending on the local market. As a general rule, however, the margin to cover adverse circumstances will be too low if the developer contributes less than:

(a) about one third of the cost of the land or its current valuation, whichever is the lower; plus

(b) one third of the cost of infrastructure—roadworks, drainage, etc; plus

(c) one half of the amount needed to finance work in progress.

Adverse circumstances, which would include such things as unforeseen additional costs or slower than expected sales, could mean increased interest charges and/or possible reductions in sales price. Accordingly, the lender needs to be entirely satisfied with the viability of the project and with the developer's drive, resourcefulness and ability, both technical and financial.

How Much Does the Developer Wish to Borrow?

(a) This has to be related to the latest audited accounts of the developer. Is the required amount too great when added to other borrowing in relation to net worth? Is effective use being made of the business's capital or is it locked into investment properties or an unduly large land bank? Builders are tempted to acquire land which they do not have the immediate resources to develop when prices are rising. However a large land bank ties up capital and raises overheads because of the need to meet interest. Ideally, therefore, a small builder with limited capital resources should not have a land bank extending much beyond two years. Three years would be an absolute maximum.

(b) Will the amount borrowed be sufficient? If the amount the lender is prepared to advance is regarded as being inadequate, the proposition should be declined.

Draw Up a Lending Plan

When the builder draws up a plan for financing the development and the lender examines it, the following points should be incorporated.

(a) It is preferable to split the lending between a building advance and a land advance (which will include infrastructure).

(b) The developer's contribution should be provided before any advance from the lender.

(c) The lending needs to be monitored to ensure that at no time does the advance exceed the agreed proportion of the costs.

(d) The building advance should be provided in stages, and a further instalment should not be provided until the lender is satisfied, either by personal site inspection or preferably by architect's certificates, that the previous instalment has produced the expected level of work in progress, and that the phasing plan is on target. The completion and selling of sites should result in a proportionate reduction in the land advance.

(e)   Whilst fluctuations will be seen in the building advance depending on the number of houses being built at a time, the objective should be to repay both the building and land advances by the time the site is, say, two thirds developed.

(f)   A charge should be taken over the land together with a simple floating charge to enable the lender to appoint a receiver to ensure that the development can be completed if problems arise.

Other Details

The lender needs to take the security, ensure that the development is adequately insured and draw up a comprehensive plan of the site, together with a schedule on which the various stages of the development can be monitored and controlled.

Monitoring and Control

Site Inspection

This needs to be done regularly and progress reports completed. A basis of assessment needs to be established of the value of work done on a partly completed house. The following scale of percentages of final cost can with the agreement of the developer and, provided the figures are realistic in the particular local situation, be used for monitoring progress.

Stages of Development of House in Course of Erection

	Percentage of cost per stage	Percentage of total cost (cumulative)
1 Damp course high	8%	8%
2 First-floor joists fixed	17%	25%
3 Roofed-in	30%	55%
4 Plastered (floors laid, door frames erected, etc.)	20%	75%
5 Glazing and plumbing finished (prime coat of paint)	17½%	92½%
6 Ready for occupation	7½%	100%

Stages of Development of Bungalow in Course of Erection

	Percentage of cost per stage	Percentage of total cost (cumulative)
1 Damp course high	10%	10%
2 Brickwork to roof-plate—joists fixed	20%	30%
3 Roofed-in	20%	50%
4 Plastered (floors laid, door frames erected, etc.)	20%	70%
5 Glazing and plumbing finished (prime coat of paint)	20%	90%
6 Ready for occupation	10%	100%

Note:

1 These percentages are based on normal conditions in the United Kingdom and will vary in particular circumstances, e.g. where more expensive foundations are essential or where higher quality final fittings are required.
2 The percentages relate to estimated costs and should not be used as a basis for security valuation.

This second point is vitally important. It is essential that the differentiation between amount of money spent and security value is understood. It is highly unlikely that work in progress will fully secure the advance even when the lending is made with a margin of at least one half. A partly finished house might be unsaleable. What the lender has to try to ensure is that when building work is completed, good and adequate security will be held.

From this, the following points emerge:

1 The lender must be confident that the borrower is an on-going business, and
2 The builder must not be allowed, under any circumstances, to start more houses than the lender has agreed to finance. To do so will increase the vulnerability of the lending and may result in more having to be lent in order to make the security saleable.

Recording and Monitoring Progress Information

The following suggestions are designed to assist with monitoring the progress of a development, particularly where more than, say, five units are being built.

The lender needs to establish standardised monitoring schedules which can be easily updated on the receipt of information from site visits or when properties are sold.

These schedules, which must be split to show the position on individual sites separately, should show:

(a) the stage reached on individual plots;
(b) the up to date cumulative value of estimated building costs and the amount advanced on building loan;
(c) the amount of land loan outstanding;
(d) overall value of security and the running limits for the land and building loans;
(e) the agreed lending plan showing the expected reductions to be achieved from each plot sale so that full repayment can be achieved at the agreed stage, usually two thirds of the way through the development.

After each site visit the schedule should be updated to give a new value for security and to show the new running limits which will then apply.

As houses are sold, the borrowing should be checked against the schedules to ensure that the lending plan agreed is proceeding as expected, or within the anticipated margin of error. The key issues will be to ensure that there is sufficient scope within the running limits to complete the development and that full repayment can still be achieved at the agreed stage.

11 PROPERTY ADVANCES

The property market tends to be cyclical, with periods of shortage and over-supply of types of building following each other. These cycles can be nationwide or merely affect a particular area. Whilst a good property developer will think well ahead, it is not uncommon for speculative developers to respond to current demand and to ignore the consequences of the time lag in building a property and getting it onto the market. In periods of excess supply, rents and property values fall before sufficient buyers/tenants are found and equilibrium is restored. When properly controlled, property lending can be both safe and remunerative, but lenders need to be very conscious of the likely market conditions, say, two years hence, and because of the difficulty in predicting, will sometimes give property lending a lower priority than lending to more stable businesses.

There are two main types of property lending:

1   Property investment. Lending is provided to purchase an existing property, with repayment coming from the rental income of the property.
2   Property development. This is, in effect, bridging finance for the borrower to purchase and develop land or property, with repayment coming from the sale of the property.

Some propositions will be a combination of both types of property advance with the completed building being let, but ownership being retained by the developer. The bridge, in such a case, would be repaid by transfer of the lending onto a term loan. Where this occurs, the lending criteria for both types of property advance will have to be satisfied.

PROPERTY INVESTMENT

When a borrower identifies an attractive investment opportunity in a property, the objective could be income yield, capital gain potential, or a combination of the two. The lender will not want the covering of the servicing costs or repayment of the advance to be dependent upon future capital appreciation of the property. The lender's assessment will concentrate on the following areas:

Rental Income/Debt Service Costs

There should be a margin of at least 15% between the rental income from the property and the interest and capital repayment cost of the lending. This margin is essential to cover situations where rental income might reduce as a result of tenants leaving or failing, or where interest rates rise. Whilst 15% will be necessary in a 'normal' situation, a lesser margin might be acceptable where a fixed rate is agreed or where the property is occupied by top class tenants, for example, a government department, committed to occupation throughout the period of the advance. The lender might accept surplus income from other charged properties to make up any shortfall in the margin against a single property.

The maintenanance of the required income/debt service cover margin needs to be specifically agreed with the borrower and incorporated as a covenant in any term loan facility letter so that there is no commitment by the lender to carry on lending if a good margin is not available.

Requests from borrowers for capital repayment holidays at the start of a loan should be rejected unless circumstances warrant such an agreement, for example, refurbishment of the property resulting in no initial income being received. Property investors often try to borrow as much as they possibly can against the income and security of their properties, and the danger of complying with capital holiday requests is that income from the property might be used to service other borrowing, with the risk that the borrower will become overstretched.

Quality of Tenants

Lessees must be capable of meeting rental payments consistently throughout the term of the lease. Lenders are generally more happy in lending for investment in commercial properties than residential buildings, which may be subject to controlled tenancies and where the landlord's rights will be more limited by legislation. The most desirable tenants will be government agencies and public companies. It would be wise to thoroughly check the standing of smaller firms or individuals through status enquiries and other means.

Conditions in the Lease

Ideally the lease should not impose any onerous obligations on the lessor, and matters such as maintenance, insurance, rates etc. should be the responsibility of the lessee. Where this is not so, as may often be the case with tenanted residential property, allowance must be made for potential expenditure when assessing the extent of income available to meet debt servicing costs.

Term of Leases

Where possible, the term of leases should be longer than the term of the lending. If this is not so, thought has to be given to the possible reduction in income should tenants not renew and replacements not be found. Even if replacement tenants appear to be readily available, there is likely to be some sort of gap in rental income which will need to be covered in the income/debt servicing margin.

Nature and Quality of the Property

The factors which will affect the attractiveness of a property to tenants and its marketability if problems occur are location, age and the number of different uses to which it can be put. A situation involving unattractive property and poor quality tenants must be avoided, especially where the term of the lease is shorter than the period of the advance.

Security Margin

The potential volatility in the value of investment property is greater than that in owner occupier property and, as a result, it is necessary to have better security cover. Depending on the quality of both the property and the tenants, cover of 150% to 200% by security of the lending will usually be appropriate.

The lending should be granted against the security of first charges, except in very exceptional circumstances. It is unlikely that good security can be provided by the equity in other lenders' security, as the margin they have assessed as being necessary in their lending may disappear in a forced sale.

Like rental income/debt service cover, the maintenance of an adequate security margin should be made a covenant in the lender's facility letter. This covenant should not only require the maintenance of the security margin, but also give the right to the lender to call for fresh valuations of a property at the borrower's expense whenever it is felt necessary.

PROPERTY DEVELOPMENT

Lending for property development is essentially the provision of bridging finance. There will be a number of uncertainties involved.

The safety of the lending will be enhanced, the more it is possible to eliminate these and make the transaction a closed bridge. The key elements in an ideal property development transaction are:

(a) The land will be available as security with detailed planning permission having been obtained.
(b) Fixed price building contract with a builder who is reputable and financially sound.
(c) Drawdown of the lending against certificates from a recognised architect or quantity surveyor.
(d) The borrower having the capacity to meet interest as it falls due so that it does not have to be added to the loan.
(e) Repayment from a reliable source, dependent only on the building work being satisfactorily completed.

Experienced developers will themselves be seeking to eliminate uncertainties and it may be possible to have a lending with all or nearly all of these ideals in place. But, frequently propositions will be received where a number of them are missing. The analysis below looks at each of the key elements and at the evaluation of the risk in lending in the circumstances of greater uncertainty which will apply.

The developer should be required to produce a detailed project appraisal, enlisting the help of professional advisers if necessary. From this, the lender can test the assumptions which the developer has made and the viability of the project.

Nature of the Security

Ideally, the property being developed will be available as security. In those circumstances where the development is to take place on land not owned by the developer, then the lender will require good alternative security or should regard the situation as being similar to that of a contract builder.

In addition to a charge on the property, consideration needs to be given as to whether a simple form of floating charge is necessary to enable the lender to defeat the appointment of an Administrator under the terms of the Insolvency Act and to be able to appoint a receiver to ensure the completion of any half finished project.

If planning permission has not been granted at the outset, the project will be extremely speculative and should only be entertained if there was both good alternative security and an alternative source of repayment.

Building Contract

An absolutely fixed price building contract is now a rare animal. A good contract builder will seek to pass on the additional costs or rises in the price of materials, etc. However fixed price contracts are by no means unknown and, in other contracts, the scope for escalation of costs can be limited. The lender's analysis of total development expenditure needs to consider a 'worst case' estimate of potential cost escalation and be satisfied that the borrower's available financial resources are sufficient to cover it. The ability of the builder to complete the contract is vital and full enquiries need to be made to establish this.

Drawdown

Drawdown of the facility must be strictly controlled, usually against the confirmation of an independent professional that work has been completed. Circumstances where tight control might be waived are when there is other good security or an alternative source of repayment.

Covering Interest

If it is necessary for interest to be added to the loan and repaid only on the sale or refinancing of the development, the lender will need to be satisfied that there is a sufficient profit margin in the transaction to cover this cost in all possible circumstances. 'Worst case' assessments will be needed of the time taken to complete and on-sell the development and of the possible effects of higher interest rates during this time.

Source of Repayment

It may be that the completed property will be sold to an owner occupier, but in many instances properties are developed for on-sale as investments. The value of a property to an investor will depend on the return it offers in comparison with other potential investments. Investing institutions will require different yields at different times depending on the quality, type and location of the property.

If a property has not been developed for a specific buyer and there is no guaranteed source of repayment, the lender will have to establish the sort of price an investor might be prepared to pay for it. The professional opinion of a good independent estate agent will give an indication of the likely yield an investor would expect from a particular property. The sale price will be a multiple of the net rental income needed to produce the required yield. For example:

>Net rent £10,000 per annum
>Required yield 10%
>Sale price £100,000

Thus, provided the level of rents at which the property can be let without difficulty is known, a conservative view can be established of a property's selling price. Knowing what this level of rents will be, again requires independent professional advice. The level of rents and likely yield which an investor will require needs to be predicted at the start of a development project which may not come to fruition for many months. The estate agent being asked to give advice needs to be someone with good knowledge of both the likely future market for properties in an area and the attitude of investors to it.

A comparison between the minimum sale price for the property and a pessimistic analysis of development costs including interest, will establish whether the proposition looks viable.

If viability looks marginal, the lender should proceed with caution. The professional advice given will have been based on the assumption that there will be a ready market for the type of property being developed. As has already been said, the character of the market is cyclical as supply and demand get out of balance, and even a good professional can get things wrong. A surplus supply of a particular type of property in an area will result in buildings lying empty for a long time and rents being depressed.

The considerable time gap between a development starting and its being put on the market makes prediction difficult, so it is important that when the property is completed, it provides a good security margin giving at least 150% cover for the lending.

Limited Recourse Property Projects

It is becoming increasingly popular to set up a special company to carry out a specific property development. This enables the borrower to isolate the risks of a development not being successful, from having an effect on the rest of the business.

The assessment of a property development proposition will be the same whether it is being undertaken as a limited recourse venture or as a normal corporate property advance. However,. where there is no or limited recourse outside the actual development, the viability of the project itself must be established beyond doubt.

A lender can be asked to provide 100% finance for a limited recourse project with the security margin being made up of unsupported guarantees from the company or companies owning the vehicle company. It may be that such guarantees will provide satisfactory security, but a great deal of care needs to be taken, for the following reasons:

(a) The guarantee will usually be from an existing property company which may already have charged its assets to secure borrowing elsewhere and/or may be from a holding company whose subsidiaries may have done the same thing. Such a guarantee would effectively be worthless.

(b) Property development companies are allowed to capitalise interest (i.e. add interest costs to other development costs to arrive at the balance sheet value of property developments) and they may have a number of other limited recourse developments in vehicle companies which do not have to be consolidated for balance sheet purposes. This can make the credit assessment of the company offering a guarantee very difficult. Just looking at the balance sheet and profit and loss figures will not be enough, and a careful scrutiny of the notes to the accounts will be required to establish the true position.

If it is not possible to be entirely satisfied with the value of guarantees offered, the lending should be limited to an acceptable proportion of the development value itself or, alternatively, the lender should insist that the guarantee being given should be supported by a tangible security.

With all limited recourse projects, a simple form of floating charge should also be taken to enable the appointment of an administrator under the terms of the Insolvency Act to be defeated and to enable a receiver to be appointed to complete any unfinished project.

12 FARMING ADVANCES

Agricultural propositions are basically no different from any other banking proposition, and the same general principles will apply. Despite this, it has not been uncommon to see farmers being allowed to borrow beyond a level they could reasonably be expected to service, simply on the assumption that land values would continue to rise. Historically, for long periods, land values have risen so that farmers have often found that their equity has increased at the same time as they have been making trading losses.

Whenever land values fall however, as they did in the mid-1980's, the need for the lender to concentrate on the serviceability of farm debt has been emphasised with a consequent proper reduction in importance being attached to current land values as security.

BACKGROUND INFORMATION AND APPRAISAL

The quality of the farm and of the farmer are vital ingredients in the commercial success of a farm business. A lender must have a detailed knowledge of both farm and farmer before starting the assessment of any proposition.

Farm

Unless thoroughly familiar with the circumstances, a visit to the farm should always be made, paying particular attention to the following, and making a detailed file note for future reference:

(a) Size—total farm acreage and effective farm acreage after deducting areas taken up by buildings, woodlands, etc.
(b) Stocking and cropping on the farm.
(c) Land type—quality and limitations to use, such as vulnerability to flooding; land classification maps will provide guidance.
(d) Layout of farm—the type of activities can be affected by the accessibility of fields. For example, dairy herds require suitable grazing within $\frac{3}{4}$ mile of the farm buildings, and outlying land is usually taken up by young stock or beef cattle.

(e) Buildings—what is the storage capacity of both stock and arable buildings? It can be useful to know the maximum number of dairy cows which can be catered for, or the quantity of grain which can be stored.

Farmer

(a) Experience—is the farmer totally familiar with the enterprises in his business, and how good is he at managing them?
(b) Are the farmer's knowledge and thinking up to date? Are modern techniques employed?
(c) Is the farmer in control to the extent of knowing what is going on in the business on a day to day basis? If he is delegating, are regular review meetings held with staff? The lender will want to talk to the individual responsible for management: for example, in the case of a dairy herd, is the farmer or the cowman in charge?
(d) How much depth is there in the management? How good is the farmer at delegating and is the next generation allowed to assume responsibility?

Farm Business

Like any other business, the commercial success of a farm business is measured in terms of financial track record. The most common source of information is the financial accounts produced for the tax authorities. Receipt of up to date accounts is often a problem with farm businesses and it is not unusual to find the last accounts are two or three years old. Obviously the older the accounts the more limited their value to the lender.

Better farmers will produce accounts more promptly. Accounts for the tax man are a useful guide, and a lender can be reasonably sure that the cost structure of the business is not underestimated. However the valuation of stock and crops can have a major impact on profitability. The best farmers are now producing management accounts for both the whole farm business and/or for important individual elements, e.g. dairying. These can provide a revealing picture of financial performance, but they should be verified against known non-financial information (e.g. total milk sales) as many farmers are not always as conscientious as they should be when completing the input forms and errors can occur.

Farmers are slowly being educated by lenders to submit budgets to support their requests for finance. The assumptions made in the budget, especially those on prices and yields, should be checked against what is known about the farm and farmer, i.e. against past performance.

The following points need to be considered:

(a) the capital structure of the business;
(b) the business's ability to service the proposed borrowing;
(c) the adequacy of the amount requested.

(a)   Capital Structure

Interpretation of the balance sheets of a farming business is essentially the same as for any other. However with farm businesses there is a further management document which can be used, known as a Farmer's Balance Sheet. This is basically a statement of the farm's assets and liabilities as assessed by the farmer. It will give an up to date assessment of the net worth of the farm business. The figures used for valuation need to be checked, but this can be readily done by, for example, examining prices given in farming magazines.

Where a new farm business is concerned, there may be little information to go on. It is vital that the overall capital structure of a new business is reasonably sound. The amount of capital needed will vary with different types of farming activity. In start up situations, it is not uncommon to find a weak capital structure and such businesses will require careful nursing by both the farmer and the lender. Whilst ideally the farm will be well capitalised, it has to be accepted that embryo businesses are likely to have a weaker capital structure and higher levels of borrowing than may be ideal.

(b)   Serviceability

There are various techniques for determining the capacity of a business to service its borrowing. The form of assessment does not have to be complicated and the simple calculation which identifies the extent of financial pressure which will be created by the proposed borrowing will be useful.

Farming activities vary widely in their level of profitability, and it is therefore inappropriate to assume that all types of business can support the same level of financial costs. A full farm budget is undoubtedly the best method of assessing lending serviceability, particularly in highly borrowed businesses. But, other more simple techniques also have a place.

(i)   Rental Equivalent

This is a popular method of assessing the financial pressure on a farm business. Whilst being a fairly crude measure, it does give a more accurate picture than some others such as 'borrowing per acre', because it embraces all financial commitments and, by doing so, removes the distinction between owner occupied and tenant farms.

The rental equivalent method expresses the cost of the land and of borrowed capital in terms of cost per effective acre. However, it does not take into account any intensive enterprises which may be on the farm as these do not use a significant amount of land.

The following financial charges will be included in the calculation:

Rent and rates
AMC interest and capital repayments
Bank overdraft interest
Interest and capital repayments on term loans
HP charges
Leasing charges
Interest on merchants' credit beyond normal trading terms
Interest and capital repayments on private loans.

Whilst the resulting figure is somewhat crude, it does give a useful guide to the financial pressure which the business has to absorb. The figure must be interpreted according to the type of farming activity being undertaken and the efficiency of the farm. Therefore, higher rental equivalents can be supported by farms with large outputs than by those with lower outputs.

The following figures represent the level of rental equivalent which would be of concern to a lender:

Specialist dairy—over £90 per effective acre.
Other land using activities—over £60 per effective acre.
Non-land using/hill and upland systems—land and finance charges over 15% of gross output.

The range of performance levels within a farming system can be much wider than the difference between farming types. The above figures show the relative profitability of dairying and cereals on a unit area basis but, generally speaking, the £60 per acre figure is a reasonable average guide above which all farmers generally must perform to remain viable.

It would however be wrong to assume that a rental equivalent of less than £60 is automatically manageable. An average rental equivalent linked to a poor performance by the farmer would still mean that a business would not be viable.

Whilst there will be a tendency for the figures to rise over time, they will not rise automatically with inflation as the servicing cost element is often the residual figure in the farm's income and expenditure. Likewise, family and large scale enterprises can support relatively higher rental equivalents than small farms with hired labour.

As has been mentioned above, rental equivalent becomes less relevant in intensive, non-land using farm enterprises, where it is better to use rental equivalent as a percentage of gross output as a measure of performance.

(ii)   Rental Equivalent as a Percentage of Gross Output

The major criticism of rental equivalent is that it ignores output. This second measure takes account of output, but requires more information. Gross output is defined as the revenue of the business adjusted for debtors, creditors and livestock purchases.

An acceptable range is 10%–15%, and anything higher than 15% would be difficult to achieve.

(iii)   Whole Farm Budgets

These are the most professional way to assess a farm's capacity to service its borrowing. Ideally the budget will be prepared on an individual basis for an individual farm with prices and yields based on the ability of that farm and that farmer. It would take account of personal drawings, tax and capital investment, whilst also reflecting the proposed cropping and stocking.

Such budgets can be prepared by farmers themselves or by accountants, consultants or an ADAS advisor. The lender, as with other businesses, will need to be satisfied that the assumptions on which the budgets are based are realistic in relation to the farm and the farmer.

Where specific information for an individual farm is not available, standard information can be used to prepare budgets. Whilst, obviously, these are not as useful as individual budgets, they are nevertheless more reliable than a rule of thumb method of assessing serviceability, such as rental equivalent.

(c)   Adequacy of Amount Requested

Ideally, a cashflow forecast will be prepared and if one is not normally produced by the farmer, it should be requested. There are many agencies to which a farmer can turn for help, not least the Farming Departments of banks who will be happy to provide assistance in this sort of area.

Generally speaking, arable farms will experience a peak requirement for cash in the July to November period, with lowest demand in the January to March period when stored harvest produce has been sold. A more even requirement for funds will be seen in dairy farming, with early summer being the low point. Distinctive peaks and troughs will occur in other livestock enterprises, coinciding with purchases and sales of animals. Sales normally occur in March/April and September/November.

Monitoring and Control of Agricultural Accounts

The drop in land prices in the mid 1980s has meant that lenders have seen a significant rise in farming failures. It has not been enough to simply expect a farmer to be able to sell a bit of land to reduce borrowing when he was in trouble. It has now become obvious that farming businesses are not 'different' and the ability to service any borrowing must be the prime consideration in looking at a farm lending. If this is in doubt, too much weight should not be placed on the current value of security.

It is prudent to pay particular attention to the following areas, reviewing the situation at least annually:

(a) The level of rental equivalent. The suggested national guidelines outlined above will be a guide, but there may be local considerations too. The lender needs to develop a knowledge of these.
(b) Is the farmer's equity less than 60% of the assets shown in the Farmer's Balance Sheet?
(c) Is a trend of negative retentions shown in the accounts?

A selective approach is needed so that the high demands of closely monitoring this kind of business are concentrated on the marginal lendings.

If any one of the above three points is unfavourable, a thorough appraisal will be called for as the potential for risk or failure will be that much greater than the norm. It would be wrong to assume that failure is inevitable, since a perfectly sound business could easily show a less than ideal position in one or even two of the areas. Nevertheless, any business which cannot satisfy all three criteria must be looked at very carefully.

Dealing with Marginal Advances

Once a farm business has given cause for concern by not meeting one of the three criteria in the previous section, or for some other reason, action needs to be taken. The precise form this will take will depend on the lender's existing knowledge of the business and surrounding circumstances. The following points represent a suggested plan for re-assessing a marginal advance:

(a) A preliminary estimate needs to be made of projected profitability.

(b) Any security held needs to be checked to ensure that it has been properly charged. The need for additional security should be considered, for example, an agricultural charge, an Agricultural Credit Corporation guarantee, etc.

(c) A review of the business should be undertaken, and the overall amount being borrowed, including from other sources of finance, should be ascertained.

(d) A farm visit is essential in order to assess viability. Any management accounts which are available should be re-assessed, and it might be necessary to request more detailed management information.

(e) A new forward budget and monthly cashflow projection should be requested. The farmer or his accountant should provide the figures, and it would be wise for the lender not to get involved in the preparation stage so that preconceptions are avoided.

(f) Assess the viability of the budget and cashflow by questioning the farmer. If unprofitable trading is being predicted, the farmer and his advisers must re-assess their underlying business plan.

(g) Consideration might be given to asking for an independent review of the farm business by some outside agency, including the bank's own Farming Department.

(h) It will be necessary to ensure that regular monitoring information of performance against budget takes place.

(i) Fix a firm date for a further review.

Security for Farm Lending

Farmers usually operate as sole traders or partnerships and the usual forms of security available from individuals can be taken to cover farming advances. There are however two special types of security which can be taken to cover a farming advance:

(a) Agricultural Charge. Under the provisions of the Agricultural Credits Act 1928, banks are able to take a charge over a farmer's assets, including both live and dead stock. Similar rights to those available in a debenture over a limited company are obtained, including the power to appoint a receiver to take over the assets and realise them if necessary.

It should be appreciated that not all of a farmer's assets may be picked up by an agricultural charge. For example, EEC milk quotas can be bought and sold, and these might represent one of a dairy farmer's most valuable assets without which the value of the farm could be significantly reduced. A milk quota is regarded as a personal asset of a farmer and, at the time of writing, is not capable of being charged.

(b) Agricultural Credit Corporation Guarantee. The ACC is a government supported body, which might be willing to provide a guarantee for a farmer's borrowing liabilities. The ACC looks to support farmers with a viable development plan, but who are having difficulty in raising finance because of a lack of security.

Readers who wish to build up a more detailed appreciation of the special requirements of lending to farmers are strongly advised to read *Finance For Farming* by Keith Checkley, published by The Chartered Institute of Bankers.

13 TRADE FINANCE

There are a number of books available which examine the technical aspects of the finance of international trade transactions, notably *Finance of International Trade* by A J W Watson, published by The Chartered Institute of Bankers. Whilst an understanding of technical matters is clearly required, the following pages concentrate on the assessment of credit risk in trade transactions.

There are inherently higher risks for businesses engaged in foreign trade than those involved in purely domestic transactions. It will be more difficult to sue overseas debtors or suppliers should things go wrong; there are potential political and exchange risks, and even transport problems, which are not present in domestic business.

Businesses engaged in international trade recognise the higher risk and this is reflected in the way that the large majority of import/export transactions are carried out. Special protective measures are used by traders to cover themselves against the dangers involved.

EXPORT FINANCE

Advances against Bills for Collection

This method of obtaining payment (outward collections) will be used by an exporter who requires greater protection than is provided by the normal domestic 'open account' method of payment, but who does not consider it necessary to go as far as to require the safeguards provided by a documentary credit.

Collections can be of two types:

1 Clean—a bill of exchange alone;
2 Documentary—a bill of exchange plus documents of title to the goods being shipped.

The lending will be made with full recourse to the exporter, whose capacity to meet any dishonoured bills plus costs and charges will be a significant issue in the credit assessment.

The advances can be made either against individual bills or a portfolio of bills. A letter of hypothecation pledging the bills as security will be necessary in both cases. A letter of hypothecation is not the best form of security as it will, for example, rank behind any debenture given to another lender. This means that if the exporter has given a prior charge over debtors, the finance would be best provided through, for example, a bills negotiated facility.

Although there will be recourse to the exporter, the primary source of repayment will be payment of the bills by the overseas buyer. The lender may be entirely satisfied that even if the overseas buyer does not pay, recourse to the exporter will ensure repayment of the debt. However, there will be instances where a great deal of reliance is put on the overseas buyer's ability to pay and, where this is so, the following considerations need to be borne in mind:

(a) What proportion of the bills should be advanced?
(b) Is there credit insurance?
(c) Will the underlying goods act as security?

Lending Proportion

It is not normal to lend 100% against the value of the bills. It is the quality of the debts which will determine the amount to be lent, and the factors which will affect quality are:

(a) Are the debts insured with ECGD or another reputable credit insurer?
(b) Is there a good spread of bills in respect of both amounts, buyers and countries? Are up to date status reports held on debtors?
(c) Has the exchange risk on currency bills been covered forward?
(d) What proportion of the debts might be affected by exchange control restrictions in overseas countries or are in countries with a poor reputation for paying?
(e) Will security be available in the form of the underlying goods?

Credit Insurance

The availability of good credit insurance for the debts will, of course, greatly improve the prospects of payment. Provided the bills are drawn for terms not more than 180 days, the exporter can obtain 90% cover on the net invoice value of each transaction under an ECGD Comprehensive Short Term policy. An assignment of this policy can be taken to boost the lender's security position. This does not make the facility full secured however, because the lender is still dependent on the exporter observing the terms and conditions of the credit insurance policy.

Goods as Security

Goods cannot be regarded as security where a collection is either clean or documents are to be released against acceptance. In such circumstances the goods will largely not be under the lender's control or will be released to the overseas buyer before payment is made.

It may be possible to get control of the goods where a collection is Documents against Payment, but the practical benefits of doing so are often questionable. When a bill is dishonoured, the goods are likely to be overseas in the importer's country. In some countries, possession of the documents of title is no guarantee of being able to obtain physical control of the goods. Even when it is possible to safely store the goods, heavy expenses are likely to be incurred and, if it becomes necessary to sell to another party, the costs of sale will further erode the proceeds. Certain goods, such as perishable or fashion goods, do not constitute good security as they are not readily saleable. Similarly, very large consignments of particular goods, especially capital goods, might be virtually impossible to sell in the event of dishonour. Costs of re-shipment back home in such a case could also be substantial and in most cases where the goods in a transaction are to be considered as security, a significant discount factor needs to be applied.

Bills Negotiated

A bills negotiated facility differs from an advance against bills held for collection in that, rather than a set percentage of a bill or bills being advanced, the lender in effect buys the bills at face value, less a discount to cover interest costs. This is in effect a 100% lending against the value of the bills. The lender retains full recourse against the exporter if the bill is dishonoured.

The credit assessment therefore will be similar to that for an advance against bills held for collection. As 100% finance is being provided, it is even more important than with a collection facility, that the underlying debtors are sound if the facility is to be regarded as completely self liquidating.

The exchange rate on bills expressed in foreign currency will be fixed at the time of negotiation, thus eliminating any exchange risk for the borrower, provided the bills are paid. In the event of dishonour however, the fact that the borrower has to provide the necessary currency to meet the liability under the recourse agreement, creates a potential exchange risk which should be considered as part of the credit assessment process.

Shorter-term Limited Recourse Facilities Secured by ECGD Policies

The withdrawal by the government of the comprehensive bank guarantees issued by ECGD to provide support for short-term export finance, has resulted in many lending institutions developing their own range of 'non-recourse' lending facilities for exporters. Although often described in this way, 'non-recourse' is a misnomer in that the lender will usually have recourse to an exporter if, for example, the overseas buyer does not pay because the goods are not up to standard and ECGD refuses to meet a claim.

Schemes of this type generally involve the advancing of 90% (although in some exceptional cases 100%) of the invoice value of exports insured by ECGD. The maximum credit period will usually be limited to 180 days, although exceptionally some schemes may allow periods of up to two years.

ECGD will provide insurance against an overseas buyer failing to pay the exporter. Normally 90% of invoice value will be paid with the exporter having to meet the balance. Where an overseas buyer defaults, the exporter will be expected to claim against his own ECGD policy to obtain the funds to repay the lender. Such claims can be expected to succeed provided the exporter has met the contractual obligations under the ECGD policy. If there are any doubts about an exporter's capacity to meet the terms of an ECGD policy there is an option open to the lender whereby the services of a company which specialises in managing exporters' ECGD policies can be used.

Similarly many banks have their own ECGD policy which can be utilised by exporters who do not have a direct relationship with ECGD themselves.

Given that the credit risk to the lender is mainly concerned with whether an exporter can meet the contractual obligations to the overseas buyer, the lender needs to look closely at the exporter's track record in performing both domestic and overseas contracts. Are the goods particularly complex to make? Is there evidence of poor quality control or past delivery dates not being met?

Provided the lender can be satisfied on these points, this kind of facility gives a strong assurance of payment from debtors and therefore generally involves less risk to the lender.

Medium-term Export Finance

Suppliers of goods of a capital or semi-capital nature can obtain finance from lenders for periods of up to 10 years with ECGD support. These advances can be made either direct to the UK supplier or indirectly by an arrangement where ECGD will provide a facility to the overseas purchaser to enable him to meet his obligations to the UK supplier. In either case, a guarantee of repayment can be provided by ECGD for up to 85% of the contract price.

It is usual for at least 15% of the contract price to be paid immediately by the overseas buyer, with the remainder being paid in instalments, usually half yearly, over the agreed credit period. The instalments will be secured by accepted bills of exchange or buyer's promissory notes.

The interest rates on these facilities are subsidised by the government and are usually very good as far as the exporter is concerned.

Whilst the lending would normally be provided in sterling, the fixed rate finance can also be made available in other hard currencies.

Forfaiting

Forfaiting is a facility available to exporters (although also being increasingly used for domestic transactions) who want to provide non-recourse credit to their overseas buyers. It is mainly used for capital goods transactions, but can also be used by exporters of raw materials and commodities.

Forfaiting works by the forfaiter purchasing, without recourse to the exporter, bills of exchange or promissory notes which represent the payment for the goods. The credit period is generally between one and five years, with the bills being drawn usually at six month intervals. The forfaiter buys the bills at a discount and then relies totally on the overseas importer to obtain repayment.

Because there is no recourse to the exporter the forfaiter will wish to be absolutely sure that the overseas buyer will pay. Thus, the ideal transaction is where the buyer is a 'blue chip' company or a government agency. Where this is not the case the forfaiter will normally look for the bills to be unconditionally guaranteed (avalised) by the buyer's bank.

Countertrade/Barter

Countertrade is the sale of goods or services to a country, where part or all of the settlement for the goods will be in the form of an agreement to buy goods/services from that country.

It is most commonly seen where exporters are dealing with countries which are short of foreign exchange, for example, Eastern Europe and the Third World. There is no generally accepted code of practice in respect of countertrade contracts, and there can be significant variations between one country and another.

IMPORT FINANCE

Documentary Credits

By issuing an irrevocable letter of credit, a bank is conditionally guaranteeing a customer's trade debt. The letter of credit represents an obligation to pay, providing that the overseas supplier meets the terms of the credit, including the provision of the documents of title to the goods being shipped.

The lender must be satisfied of the buyer's ability to meet the liability on the due date, and if any doubts persist about this, then full or partial cash cover should be taken from the buyer at the time the letter of credit is issued. It must be understood that once an irrevocable letter of credit is in existence, all the overseas supplier has to do is meet its terms and conditions, and the lender will be obliged to pay.

Goods as Security

Some lenders profess that documentary credit facilities involve less risk than ordinary borrowing liabilities because the lender can look to the underlying goods as security. This can be a dangerous misunderstanding.

The lender's liability under a letter of credit can be secured by the goods being imported, provided control can be exercised over them and there will be a ready market for them should the importer not be able to meet the obligation. The following circumstances must therefore apply:

(a) The terms of the letter of credit must provide for documents to be released against payment and not against acceptance, as in the latter case the lender would lose control of the goods when they were released to the importer on acceptance of a bill.

(b) There must be a ready market for the goods outside the confines of the particular transaction. This might not be the case where, for example, perishable, fashion, capital or specialist goods are involved. The difference between invoice value and a likely forced sale value ought to be covered by a cash margin, which should also take into account storage and selling costs. Only in this way could the facility be regarded as being fully secured and self-liquidating.

(c) The documents must enable the lender to acquire title to the goods. This means a full set of shipping documents in negotiable form, including clean, on-board bills of lading, blank endorsed and marked 'freight paid'. Shipments covered by airways bills or lorry consignment notes cannot be regarded as secured as such documents are not documents of title.

(d) As the lender will not deal in the actual goods, but only in the documents relating to those goods, it is important to be satisfied that the overseas supplier will ship them as prescribed in the credit. If the supplier's integrity is in doubt, it would be wise for a certificate of inspection to be included as a provision in the terms of the credit.

(e) The goods must be fully insured.

(f) Any import licence requirements should have been covered by the importer.

(g) If the credit is expressed in foreign currency, the possible exchange risk involved in selling the goods in sterling needs to be taken into account.

Avalising

Avalising involves adding the lender's name to a bill or promissory note on behalf of the drawee, giving the effect of 'guaranteeing' payment. An importer is therefore able to get his bank to unconditionally guarantee a debt to an overseas (or domestic) supplier.

Avalising is mainly used when dealing with European suppliers. Its use is much more widespread on the Continent than it is in the United Kingdom and its status under English law is obscure. Lenders will therefore be wise to take a counter-indemnity from their customer to ensure they have a right of recourse should the customer fail to meet the primary obligation on the bill.

If the bill is expressed in foreign currency, the lender will have a potential exchange risk in having to convert sterling into the currency to meet it.

EXCHANGE RISK

Forward Contracts

Transactions involving a foreign currency always carry the risk that adverse movements in exchange rates may result in less sterling being received or more having to be paid than originally calculated. The risk can be eliminated by using forward contracts, which fix at the outset the exchange rate on a future transaction. This rate is not then affected by subsequent movements in the spot rate for the particular currency.

A lender faces two main types of risk in relation to foreign exchange transactions, both spot and forward.

(a) Settlement Risk. This occurs where payment instructions are given by a customer in such a way that the bank pays away currency before reimbursement in sterling can be obtained from the customer. Thus a bank may be at risk for the full face value of the remittance, albeit for only two or three days.

(b) Marginal Risk. This arises when a forward contract has to be liquidated resulting in either a profit or loss, depending on the spot rate at the time of liquidation. A loss will mean that the customer's liability to the bank is increased by the amount of the loss. Some lenders regard the marginal risk on currency transactions as being so potentially small that it can be totally ignored. Others, however, apply formulae in which they assess the risk against individual transactions as a percentage of the contract amount. Given that exchange rates may fluctuate more over longer periods, these percentages tend to increase, the longer the term of the contract.

Currency Options

A major disadvantage of forward contracts from a customer's point of view, is that whilst the fixed exchange rate guards against adverse currency movements, the customer is not able to take advantage of favourable movements. A currency option contract however allows this.

The holder of an option contract has the right, but not the obligation, to buy or sell a specified amount of currency at an agreed rate within a specified period. A fee is paid for this right.

Tender to Contract Cover

Businesses engaged in activities which require them to submit a tender a long time in advance of a contract being started have a particularly difficult exchange risk management problem. The price they quote now in foreign currency may give them a good profit on a potential contract, but currency movements by the time the contract is due to start may wipe this out. However if they fix the currency rate now they may not win the contract and thus be involved in a loss in closing out a forward exchange deal. Many banks now offer tender to contract cover to deal with this problem.

At the time of tendering, the company agrees with the bank a schedule of forward contracts, designed to cover the exchange risk on the receivables arising out of the contract. This enables the company to build into budgets reliable figures for income from the contract.

A front-end, non-returnable fee is charged, for which the bank agrees to open the necessary forward contracts, but only if the company is successful in its tender. The customer is obliged to take out foward cover with the bank at the agreed exchange rates, but if the tender is unsuccessful, the facility is automatically cancelled.

Tender to contract cover is essentially a mix of forward contracts and currency options, and is one representative of a large number of ways of hedging currency exposure being developed by banks and other institutions to cover exchange risk.

INDEX